The
Princess
Within

SERITA ANN JAKES

Foreword by **T. D. Jakes**

The
Princess
Within

Restoring the Soul of a Woman

BETHANYHOUSE
Minneapolis, Minnesota

The Library of Congress has cataloged the original edition as follows:
Jakes, Serita Ann.
    The princess within : restoring the soul of a woman / by Serita Ann Jakes.
        p. cm.
    ISBN 1-57778-101-5 (hardback) — ISBN 0-7642-2747-5 (pbk)
    1. Christian women—Religious life. 2. Women—Conduct of life. I. Title.
BV4527.J345 1999
248.8'—dc21
                                                                    2001274505

Dedication

These pages are penned
with precious memories of Mother,
who now is resting safely
in the arms of the Secret Keeper,
To my children, whose love beckons me
beyond my past into my future, and
To my husband, my friend,
my prince to whose hands I cling
to keep my heart from falling.

Acknowledgments

Thank you, June Brown (Albury Publishing)
for coming to find me so that
this testimony could be delivered to many
and I could find my shoe.

Cristine Bolley (Wings Unlimited),
your heart for ministry was deeply expressed
as you joined me in believing that fairy tales do come true.

Albury Publishing, thanks for being the carriage
that drove *The Princess Within*.

Finally, to my extended family
who encouraged me throughout this project,
Let the celebration begin!

Contents

$\mathcal{M}$emories, how they linger
How they ever flood my soul.
In the stillness of the midnight,
Sacred secrets still unfold . . .

Therefore if any woman be in Christ,
she is a new creature:
old things are passed away;
behold, all things are become new.

2 CORINTHIANS 5:17

(AUTHOR'S PARAPHRASE)

Foreword

Way back in a hollow in the back woods of West Virginia, somewhere over a rope bridge traversing a mountain creek, lived my Serita. A young diamond set among mountains of coal, she was a girl whose life would grow and become multifaceted through pressures without and godly influences within. Then one day, when she reached the full flower of womanhood, she became the one I sought for: flesh of my flesh and bone of my bone, my Nubian princess, my lover, my friend, a jewel by my side to reflect the radiance of the Master. Her confidence now strengthens me and moves me on when I am tired. Her joy brings a smile to my face when I am low. Her playfulness keeps my child's heart alive. She is my glory! When she is flourishing, I prosper; and God looks good. Ever since the day we became one flesh, I have entrusted my heart in Serita's hands. Now, in commending her to you, I entrust you to her also.

As a pastor, it means a lot to me to know that the women of my church are finding out who they are in Christ. It is important for them to be strengthened in their faith as they represent over half the number of those who attend our church, The Potter's House in Dallas, Texas, and an even larger percentage of the global church. I have watched and listened as my wife has ministered to women at home and around the country. Her heart, like mine, is to see women healed, strengthened, and renewed. Her message is that, as a woman of God, there is a place for you beyond feelings of helplessness, aimlessness, or hopelessness. Strength and confidence can be your life foundation as you discover the Father's presence in the pressures and influences of your daily routine.

If you are finding it hard to forget the woman you used to be before you gave your life to Jesus, then please read this book. If the woman you were behaved in unthinkable ways and is now blocking your view of God's love for you, then let Serita, as a sister in the faith, show you how God sees you through Christ. As she shows you how He has worked so faithfully in her walk, I trust you will reflect on how He has shown His power and grace in your life. Or, where your life is like a scratched or marred diamond, or is missing the full-faceted splendor that God intends for you, let her words and testimony impart to you both the future and the hope that are yours in Christ.

I thank God that my wife felt it was important to write this timely message. There is a rich deposit within her heart that she has exposed for your benefit. The fine lace and satin that clothes her frame, her silk purse, and her regal coiffure are but a well-tooled cover to a book that holds many chapters of brokenness and loss, love and laughter, abundance and lack. It is because she has allowed God to pour oil, spikenard, and myrrh through the chapters of her life that He has turned her ashes into beauty, her mourning into joy, and now has allowed her to aromatize the lives of others.

God bless you as you read, ponder, and pray; and may your life, like a precious stone, reflect the fullness of His faithfulness, grace, mercy, and love in your life.

T.D. JAKES

*A*nd he that sat upon the throne said,
Behold, I make all things new.
And he said unto me,
Write: for these words are true and faithful.

REVELATION 21:5 KJV

Is This Book for You?

*E*very woman was born to be a princess. Our Father, God in heaven, is the ruler over all the earth. As His children, adopted into His family through our faith in Jesus Christ, the King of Kings, we are royal heirs to all of God's promises. Our Creator designed His daughters to be the glory of men and the mothers of all living things. We were the final touch of creation and the solution to loneliness in mankind. Why have so many women fallen from that place of honor and esteem?

It grieves me to see women hiding in the shadows of a busy church, shamed and saddened by sacred secrets from their past they wish to conceal. Christian women should be restored to their place of wholeness before God so their testimony will draw all women back to the Lord. Yet many beautiful Christian women are still trying to keep their secrets instead of giving them to the Lord, their Secret Keeper.

The dirt of their old lives clings to them as if they bathe in liquid silt each morning. They go about their daily routine covered with fresh mud, concealing their true identity, pretending not to even notice their filthy condition. Their light is not shining, and no one can see the princess within whom their

Father created them to be. All signs of their royal inheritance have been covered with the degradation of mistakes that were made at some point in their lives.

These women are like Cinderella. Even after giving their lives to Jesus, being fully aware of their rightful inheritance, they continue to retreat to the corners and dust themselves with the cinders of the ash heap. Are you like her?

Wicked oppressors tried to make Cinderella ashamed of her humble position, convincing her that she was not worthy to participate in the celebrations of the kingdom. When the truth came that she could indeed go to the ball, she had to lift her chin, regain her dignity, and dress herself with attire more befitting a woman ready to offer her hand to a prince.

Have you put on wedding clothes since you were adopted into the family of God?

Are you waiting for someone to give you a ride to the celebration, or will you find your own way to the dance as Cinderella did?

Are you willing to be obedient to the One who redeemed you to your rightful place, even to the point of leaving behind your beautiful shoe?

Once Cinderella became joint-heir with her prince, she used her good fortune to help others. How did this all come about for her? Her humility and willingness to serve positioned her for blessing, and once she understood who she really was, her passion to serve others was empowered by the king.

A prince waited to find Cinderella.

A Prince of Peace awaits you.

There are critics who say that life is not like fairy tales with happy endings. I write this book to prove otherwise. I have been like Cinderella, and I am convinced through a working of the Holy Spirit, who is whispering within me, that you are like her too. Each chapter will examine the phases of our growth from shame to spiritual maturity. We will see how to move from the cinders of our past to the celebration of our future.

Will you be free of your past and enjoy all that God has for you?

Will you let His truth cleanse you from the secrets to which you remain in bondage?

Will you learn to give your secrets to your precious Secret Keeper?

When I gave my secrets to the Secret Keeper, He replied with words that made the secrets lose their power over me. He released the woman within me to walk with dignity, not because of who I was, but because of who my Father is. If we are not condemned before God, where is the shame?

It is time for all women to be restored to this place of honor that God first intended for them to have. He gave women the power to help men enjoy His presence. We must be restored to that relationship with God if we are to be an influence on mankind to do the same.

My husband, Bishop T.D. Jakes, author of *Woman, Thou Art Loosed,* teaches in his recent *New York Times* bestselling title *The Lady, Her Lover, and Her Lord,* that it is crucial for every woman to find balance in her life and fulfillment in her heart. He says it is "the duty of every man to help his lady achieve her greatness."

I believe that God has gifted women with the power to influence the men in their lives to action. I also believe it is the opportunity of every woman to give her husband the courage to believe for impossible things through Jesus Christ. However, she can take this gift that was meant to be a positive reinforcement to a man's faith and misuse it to pull him down. When Christian women are no longer deceived, when we fully understand who we are in Christ, our gift of influence will lead our men and children back to God's promise. But we must first find the truth ourselves, before we can light the way for others.

My prayer for writing this book is to demonstrate God's power to remove the shame of our deception and to restore the joy of our royal inheritance. When we find this balance and fulfillment that my husband speaks of in his books, we will lead our families to an intimate encounter with the Father.

It is time to forget the woman you used to be. God has forgotten her. It is time to prepare for the great celebration that our King of Kings is planning for us. Come away from the cinders, and please stay with me through the end of the book. Spend this time with me as I tell you my own story of discovering *The Princess Within*.

Love,
Serita Ann

If we confess our sins, he is faithful and just
and will forgive us our sins
and purify us from all unrighteousness.

1 JOHN 1:9

CHAPTER
One

Princess, Why Are You Hiding?

LIFE IS LIKE A FAIRY TALE!

*Cinderella forgot that she was the rightful heir to her
father's fortune. Shamed into servanthood, she allowed
her inheritance to be squandered by unworthy benefactors.
Have you forfeited what your Father in heaven
has written in His will for you?*

Once upon a time, not so very long ago, a beautiful daughter
was born to the King of all kings, and the Lord of all lords. Her
father loved her and attended to her needs as if she were his only
child. His greatest hope was that she would grow to understand
how very much he loved her.

The King was a good king and used his wealth to provide
for all the people in his kingdom. He hoped that one day his
beautiful daughter would help him to demonstrate his love for
his people.

This powerful king had an evil enemy who hated the king
and all that was his. Those who encountered the King's enemy

referred to him as the Evil One. The Evil One wanted to hurt the King, but knowing he was invincible, the Evil One tried to hurt the King's daughter instead. Disguised as a prince, the Evil One came to the daughter to court her and win her trust away from the King.

This Evil Prince used cunning flattery to draw her away from the protection of the King's castle by promising to give her all the things for which her father had asked her to wait. She followed the Evil Prince, and once he had her in his clutches, he robbed her of her most precious gift—her dignity.

The Evil Prince dressed her in rags, smeared her face with ashes, and stood her before his evil followers, who mocked her and called her names. Shamed before the contemptuous crowd, the beautiful princess retreated to the dungeon, where the Evil Prince had told her she belonged. She forgot the words of her father, and only remembered the humiliation of standing in public view and feeling naked and ashamed. She vowed to herself that if she ever went outside of her dungeon, she would disguise her true identity so the crowd would never mock her again.

From that day on she covered her beautiful face whenever she ventured out of her secluded hiding place. The Evil Prince had convinced her that she was unworthy, unloved, and unwanted. He had separated her from her father and gloated in his apparent victory to hurt the King by making the princess ashamed of who she was. Her secret humiliation kept her imprisoned by the evil enemy who had tricked her with his lies.

Secrets create invisible strongholds

Perhaps you know how the princess in this story feels. Perhaps her story sounds just like yours. I know it sounds like my story. The devil's only weapons against God's children are his lies, but he fires them against us with relentless force. If we know to hide behind God's shield of truth, we will not fall subject to these lies. But if we listen to the devil's lies, we will become afraid of God and want to hide from Him.

It is difficult to love God or anyone else when we are looking for a hiding place. Shameful secrets cause us to withdraw in fear that someone will bring our experience to the knowledge of others. Intimidation is a dark and dreary place in which to live. Even when light penetrates our room, we look for dark corners in which to retreat so we can keep our secrets from exposure.

Hiding feels comfortable at the time, but it is a lonely lifestyle to maintain. If secrets are allowed to run the course of their destruction, finding new ways to keep these secrets can become more sacred than our search for freedom from them. There is hope, however, for people who find a trustworthy friend to whom they can tell their secrets. Many people have found healing by revealing their secrets to a person who can demonstrate forgiveness to them. Secrets lose their power if there is no longer a reason to hide their truths. The right secret keeper can make the person feel acceptable again.

This need for the acceptance of others drives us to great measures because we tend to agree with the opinions that others have of us. If our peers want to imitate us, we are flattered. If they make fun of us, we are defeated. We must be careful whom we choose to be our secret keeper. If we tell our secret to the wrong person, they might use it against us and inflict more shame on us than we previously carried. But it is also true that if we share a secret with someone who accepts us for the new person in Christ that we are becoming, we find liberation from our guilt and enjoy new beginnings.

Love covers a multitude of sins

I am careful with secrets that others give to me. It is my way of showing them that I accept them as they are. My confidence in them helps to relieve their sense of shame as they accept my love in spite of what has happened to them or what they have done. I am not concerned about the choices they made in their past, but in the choices they will make in the future. I have learned this art of secret keeping from God, who has been faithful to keep my own secrets, secrets that intimidated me and kept me from enjoying the new life He gave to me.

We have nearly 10,000 women enrolled in our Dallas church, The Potter's House. I see many who are reluctant to participate in the move of God because they have secrets that they feel are worse than those of any other woman. It is in my heart to reveal how the Lord has been my Secret Keeper in hopes that all women who read my story will also learn to trust their secrets to Him.

I know that secrets rob us of the freedom we have to enjoy our royal inheritance through Jesus Christ. I too have hidden behind appropriate smiles when inappropriate pain robbed me of my right to be content. I was afraid of my future because of my past until I met my Lord, my Secret Keeper. I am proof that the Lord can be trusted to keep secrets. Once I gave to Him the secrets that kept me from being totally His, I found that those same secrets were now totally His to keep. He removed the shame that I felt and covered me with His truth and love again. His love made me transparent, with nothing to hide.

I have found healing by writing letters to the Lord, my Secret Keeper. The act of explaining my fears and waiting on God to respond has taken me to a place of solitude with Him where He can speak to me and direct my thoughts to His Word. When I felt troubled about the loss of my brother, and a subsequent encounter I had with a young man that I dated shortly after my brother's death, I wrote the following letter (p. 30) to my Secret Keeper. I was honest before God and He was faithful to show me truths that set me free from the pain of those memories.

As I began to write this letter to Him, I remembered the passage of Scripture from Genesis 32:24:

> So Jacob was left alone, and a man wrestled with him till daybreak.

Jacob was afraid that his own brother, Esau, was going to kill him because he had tricked him out of his birthright. By going before God, Jacob laid his fears before his Lord and requested deliverance from the things that kept him from receiving God's promises. In answer to his prayers, an angel came and wrestled with Jacob until daybreak. Once Jacob realized that he was strong enough to wrestle all night with an angel, who in the end blessed him, he realized that it was foolish to fear his brother who was merely a man.

Through that midnight struggle, God put strength into Jacob that he could not have developed without that encounter. Even though Jacob left limping, he was no longer afraid of the challenges a new day brought to him. Like Jacob, when it was time for me to let God heal my infirmities, I laid my grief before God to see what His healing power could do.

You are not alone if you have sacred secrets that shame you from participating in the great things God has planned for you, but it is time for you to confess to God the truth of your secret so that He can free you from your past.

I had wanted to hide as a teenager because of the shame I felt when a violent boyfriend rejected me. His actions toward me made me feel unlovely, unwanted, and jilted. I hid this sense of rejection for many years, not realizing how much it affected me until I took time to be honest before God and admit my secret pain to Him. I was free from the secret after writing a letter to my Lord. Once I told Him how I felt and saw how much He loved me, the event lost its power to hurt me. It even seems odd now that I ever felt it was a secret worth keeping. I wrote,

Dear Secret Keeper,

I think that being young and naïve often creates a canvas for You to show us how You paint Your master plan for our lives. All I can say is that I believed him. He had been so nice. He picked me up from school every day. Even the gifts he brought to me were such a surprise. What went wrong? At first I didn't notice his weaknesses, because he seemed to be such a strong man.

It was right after my brother had died. No, let me correct that statement. It was right after my brother was murdered. My whole world seemed to come to a screeching halt. How could his

life be ended so abruptly, just when he was trying to get it all together? He had given his life to You. For the first time in his life, my brother seemed to have found true happiness—the kind of happiness that I knew (even then) only came from having You as the center of his life.

One evening he went out with his daughters to one of the local hangouts. The girls were raising money for a trip to an amusement park, and their daddy was taking them where all of his friends would be. Everybody liked my brother, I thought. But something went wrong. There was an argument. Then there were gunshots, and my brother tumbled to the bottom of the stairs.

His knees were drawn to his chest in the fetal position, but this was not his entrance into life. It was his tragic exit. When they took our mother to him, she went into shock. Her firstborn was gone, and she was left alone.

Oh, Secret Keeper, I was looking for my brother! I was looking for someone who enjoyed having fun like my brother. But instead, I found him. He liked to have fun, but sometimes he seemed so angry. I began to notice bouts of anger that soon became hostility toward me. The hostility turned into verbal outbursts that I could not believe my ears were hearing. As suddenly as it happened, he would return to being the person I had grown so fond of.

He visited every day. I even recognized the sound of his car when he drove up. But the visits became shorter; there was always something else he had to do. As the visits grew briefer, the atmosphere became more intense and often resulted in senseless arguments. I felt like something wasn't right. I could almost sense danger every time he came.

In my heart, I felt warned that the relationship was taking a turn for the worse. I heard his car, but he didn't stop one day.

Then I heard his car as he passed without stopping a second day. When he finally decided to stop and come in, he accused me as if I had done something wrong. I was so amazed that I had sat there for several days waiting for someone who I thought really cared for me. The accusations turned into rage. The rage turned into threats of violence. What game was this we played?

My Secret Keeper stopped me from continuing by pouring into my soul the memory of His promise from Psalm 121:1–8. I looked up the scripture and read it to myself as though the Lord were speaking it directly to me. Such a paraphrase reads like this:

Dear Serita Ann,

You will lift up your eyes to the hills—where does your help come from? Your help comes from Me, the Lord, the Maker of heaven and earth.

I will not let your foot slip—I who watch over you will not slumber; indeed, I who watch over Israel will neither slumber nor sleep. I, the Lord, watch over you—I am your shade at your right hand; the sun will not harm you by day, nor the moon by night.

I, the Lord, will keep you from all harm—I will watch over your life; I, the Lord, will watch over your coming and going both now and forevermore.

My Lord had wrestled with me just as He had done with Jacob. Though I had been weakened by the young man who pulled down my countenance, my Lord strengthened me with the memory that He was always there with me. I returned to my writing and finished telling my Lord the secret that had haunted me.

I don't know why I didn't heed the warning that You gave to me. I knew that things were about to come to a boil. Whenever I heard his car, I became nervous. It had been nearly a week. There had been neither phone calls nor visits. If history was to be repeated, I knew that when he did return he would be very hateful.

The day he finally came again, he left his opinion of me written on my heart. He destroyed my sense of value that day. He made me feel ashamed for being me. I relived the day in my letter to my Secret Keeper:

It sounds like the car has stopped. Why is he walking so fast? Oh please, no arguing again. "But I haven't been anywhere!" I remember saying.

It hurts when he shoves like this.

Why is he pushing me?

Is that a gun in his hand?

What is he doing?

I've never seen such a face; it's like looking at the devil himself. Is he going to kill me, Secret Keeper? He's got his gun to my head, and I'm lying on the floor. God, help me!!!

This poor man called, and the Lord heard him; he saved him out of all his troubles.

The angel of the Lord encamps around those who fear him, and he delivers them.

PSALM 34:6–7

I looked up and he was gone. I crawled to the window and peeked under the shade. He stood there beneath the full moon, cocked the gun and fired it into the air five times. I sat on the floor trembling; tears would not come. Everything that I thought he was had turned to lies. When I met him, I felt so lonely. When he drove off, again I felt left alone.

    But then I realized that I had not been left alone. I had called out to You, and You had sent an angel to rescue me from death! I'm never alone because I always have You, Secret Keeper.

                Love,

                Serita Ann

In this last event, I was merely the victim, but I felt exposed. Over a course of time I began to believe that I must have deserved this treatment. I believed the lie and was tormented by his opinion of me. He had stripped me of my sense of self-worth and had robbed me of my dignity. But now, after laying my secret before the Lord, after wrestling with the truth that God was there protecting me and saving me from further harm, I am no longer ashamed. I no longer limp from the wounds the enemy of God inflicted upon me. I no longer believe that lie . . . and I am free to love again.

The Lord is the best Secret Keeper of all. I confessed my secret shame to Him: I had fallen for the wrong person. I had ignored His warnings, but He took my honesty and my fears and cleansed me, sending my secret away as though it had never happened. What is this power He offers?

What is this power that comes from Jesus' death and makes us live? He paid a price in that death for every secret that we hide so that we can stand justified before God. Evangelists explain "justified" as "Just as if I'd never done it—just as if it had never happened to me."

Why keep our secrets to ourselves instead of giving them to the Lord, our Secret Keeper and trusted friend? With Jesus we can come out of hiding.

What secrets are you hiding?

What secrets are keeping you from enjoying new opportunities that lie ahead? You are not alone if you have sacred secrets that shame you from participating in the great things God has planned for you, but it is time for you to confess to God the truth of your secret so that He can free you from your past. It is time for you to enjoy your inheritance, which is to be purified from all unrighteousness.

> If we confess our sins, he is faithful and just and will forgive us our sins and purify us from all unrighteousness.
>
> 1 JOHN 1:9

For us, "purify" means "to make pure again." God offers more than forgiveness to us. He offers the power to make us free from what *Webster's New World Dictionary* defines as "adulterating matter." When lies and mistakes enter our otherwise pure lives, we become a mixture of good and evil, we are *adulterated* by the adding of the bad to the good that God made in the beginning. Reversing this, God takes our secrets and restores our innocence, freeing us from the evil of sin and its corrupting elements. Through our confession, we allow God to cleanse us from anything that is not right in our lives.

There is no secret that can separate you from God's love.

There is no secret that can separate you from His blessings. There is no secret that is worth keeping from His grace.

God has already provided deliverance for all that you have done and all that has been done to you. He has demonstrated His love from the beginning of time, and He continues faithfully to reach out to you even this very second in time as you read this book.

Confess your secrets to the Lord, your Secret Keeper. Let Him make right the things in your life that cause you to retreat. You are no longer a lady-in-waiting or a lady-in-hiding. You are a princess!

Write your own story

Before we continue, I would like to make a suggestion. Writing out your feelings will help you to see what the Lord already knows about you. So why not write a letter to the Lord, your Secret Keeper, in your journal. Each time you write, tell Him what secret makes you want to hide.

When you finish each letter, ask Him what He thinks about your secret. Then listen to His still, small voice within your heart and record His response in your journal.

But as many as received him, to them gave he power to become the sons [daughters] of God, even to them that believe on his name.

JOHN 1:12 KJV

CHAPTER
Two

But Everyone Is Invited to the Party!

LIFE IS LIKE A FAIRY TALE!

Cinderella believed that everyone in the entire kingdom was entitled to go to the ball except her. Without an argument she agreed to stay home, even though she had a great desire to see the Prince. What or who is keeping you at home?

Cinderella's mean stepsisters told her that she wasn't invited to the ball. At first, she believed them and planned to stay at home. *After all,* she thought, *who would want to dance with a servant girl?* If she had continued to listen to the lies, what were Cinderella's chances of living happily ever?

Have you ever heard of a party that a friend was having, but you didn't know for sure if you were invited? Perhaps a general announcement was made at work or at church, but you didn't hear it. When an associate asked if you were going, you were too embarrassed to admit that you didn't think you were on the guest list, so you just said, "No, I'm not going." Perhaps you were too proud to find out for sure if you were to be included, so you said that you had plans for that day. What makes us so willing to be left out?

It hurts me to see women hiding in the shadows because they feel left out. In a church as large as ours, it is difficult to personally reach each woman and invite her to participate in what we have planned. How I long to see the day when women are restored to the place God esteemed for them, when they boldly come to the forefront to celebrate their position in His kingdom!

God looks at each of us as if we were His only daughter. And of course, He wants us to be included in all He is doing. He doesn't want us to lie to ourselves about that. But people are not always like God, and they often do things that make us feel left out.

Feeling left out can fill us with a sense of shame. It's difficult to admit that we feel hurt when our peers do not include us, so we keep our pain of being excluded a secret. But what would happen if we told our Secret Keeper how we felt? What would He say to us if we would quiet ourselves before Him after admitting our shame to Him?

I have felt left out before, so I wrote to my Lord, and my Secret Keeper:

Dear Secret Keeper,

Why are we so cruel to one another? I've always been a somewhat sensitive person. Whatever I felt, I would feel to the third power. I tried desperately not to say or do anything that would make anyone feel less than me. I wanted to get along with everyone and could never understand why two people could not share the same friend. I didn't want to say words to others that I would not want said to me. I never believed the old saying, "Sticks and stones may break my bones, but words will never harm me." I knew how vicious the mouths of insensitive people could be.

Even as a child, I learned that insensitive remarks inflicted pain. I often felt that I was the target of most of the darts of humiliation. I can still feel some of the pain from those who would chant, "Fatty, fatty, two-by-four!" These were the children that I wanted most to impress. I wasn't athletic, but was forever trying to be selected for the neighborhood sporting events. My dresses often looked like they were designed for someone much older because the chubby selections of the mail order catalogues were very limited.

In my eyes, everyone looked like they could model for Seventeen Magazine. *They all were tall with long legs, unlike me, who was the runt of the litter and as wide as I was tall. No one would accept me but my mama, who indulged me with her sweet potato pies and chocolate cakes. She understood that I was a growing girl.*

I thought the other girls who had called me names were so beautiful. Somehow they were the epitome of all I ever hoped to be—thin. I set out to become just like them. I ran extra laps during physical education class and made sure I did twice as many sit-ups. I did so many jumping jacks that for minutes later I felt as though I were a windmill. I even said no to all of Mama's goodies. All of this was to no avail.

After losing a few pounds, all I became was sore and hungry. I still wasn't one of "them." I wasn't like them. It wasn't only the outside that I couldn't match; it was something emanating from the inside. It was their spirit. They were beautiful outwardly, but there was something very rotten inside of them. Suddenly I realized that I didn't want to be like them after all. Physically, they were all I aspired to be, but the lost condition of their souls overwhelmed that outward beauty.

Yes, I was fat on the outside, but they were ugly on the inside. I could go on a diet; they would need far more than a charm course.

Realizing this truth, I began to take inventory of myself, and an invaluable transformation took place in my self-esteem. I suddenly realized that beauty is not just expressed outwardly. Beauty is more than how you look. Beauty is in how you accept others for who they are. It comes from inside no matter what the image in the mirror suggests or what society dictates.

Beauty is You, Secret Keeper. You continually look beyond my flaws and meet my needs. Now when I look for a role model or someone to imitate, I look into the mirror of Your Word. I behold palely the image that You are creating, and I shed secret tears because I can hardly believe that this is how You see me.

Love,
Serita Ann

I remembered the words of my Lord in Matthew 23:27–28 when He said,

Woe to you, teachers of the law and Pharisees, you hypocrites!
You are like whitewashed tombs, which look beautiful on the outside but on the inside are full of dead men's bones and everything unclean.

In the same way, on the outside you appear to people as righteous but on the inside you are full of hypocrisy and wickedness.

Obviously, the Lord is also grieved by insensitive people who act piously while making others feel worthless and insignificant. He too longs for His truth to be made known to us. He is planning a party to celebrate the union of His Son, Jesus, and His bride, the Church. Everyone is invited, but an RSVP is necessary.

A general announcement has been made throughout the Scriptures, but many people still have not heard about the party He has planned. Many of those who have heard don't understand that this party is very real. In fact, that day of celebration is closer to us with each new day.

Please RSVP!

When John the disciple had a revelation of Jesus Christ, the angel who was with him said, *Blessed are they which are called unto the marriage supper of the Lamb.* The angel continued, *These are the true sayings of God* (Revelation 19:9 KJV). The revelation recorded in the last book of the Bible was a record of the things that would come to pass in the future. We know that God wants everyone to come to the party. He is not willing that any should perish, but that all should respond to His invitation.

In the Bible, Peter explains how the RSVP works.

The Lord is not slow in keeping his promise, as some understand slowness. He is patient with you, not wanting anyone to perish, but everyone to come to repentance.

2 Peter 3:9

God wants all of us to come to repentance. By grace, He is delaying the beginning of the dance in order to give us all time to come forth and accept His invitation to be a part of that great reunion.

There is room at God's house for everyone who is willing to come. John confirms this in his gospel:

> But as many as received him, to them gave he power
> to become the sons [daughters] of God, even to them
> that believe on his name.

John 1:12 kjv

We only have to acknowledge receipt of the invitation, and all that God has to offer becomes ours.

Many people look at the coming of Jesus Christ as something far in the future. While writing this book, a hurricane swept across Central America, causing floods and mud slides throughout the countryside. The death toll in Honduras may be impossible to accurately assess, but so far, we know that Jesus came for at least seven thousand people in just one day. I hope the people in Honduras responded favorably to the wedding invitation. An entire community now knows the reality of the party that Jesus has planned for those who have received Him.

God's faithfulness is so dependable, it will fill you with awe to discover how much He loves you. His love is unconditional, meaning He *always* loves you, not just when you do something right. No matter what you do, no matter who you do it with, God still loves you. Does that sound like a love that only happens in fairy tales?

Well, Cinderella's story doesn't compare to the happiness God has planned for you. Daily He invites you to come to His garden party and visit with Him in the cool of the evening, just as He first did with Adam and Eve. He's waiting for you now. (See Genesis 3.)

What keeps us from going to our Lord and sharing our secrets with Him? The self-punitive tendency to hide from God when we feel ashamed is inherited from our parents, Adam and Eve. From the beginning, God enjoyed meeting His children for an evening talk. God extended a standing invitation to meet in the garden where Adam and Eve could walk with Him and enjoy the fellowship of His wonderful presence. This daily garden party would have continued for their children and eventually for us, but Adam and Eve stopped going to the party because they were ashamed of what they had done and of what had been done to them.

Eve had believed a lie, and when it came time to meet with God for her evening embrace, she wanted to hide from Him instead. But God continues to invite us into His presence and has made a way for us to escape the penalty of our fallen nature. We can be restored to the relationship with Him that He originally planned for all women. We can learn of God's original plan for us through Eve's story.

The life God had planned for Eve was what we would now call a fairy tale. Her husband adored her and he listened to her every whim and fancy. She was a perfect "ten" in his eyes. They were in such agreement that they were known by the same name, Mr. and Mrs. Adam. Because they were one with each other, there was no need to identify him independently from her. What she wanted, he wanted. Their union was a picture of the communion they had with God.

Cinderella's story doesn't compare to the happiness God has planned for you. Daily He invites you to come to His garden party and visit with Him in the cool of the evening, just as He first did with Adam and Eve. He's waiting for you now.

Their wealth surpassed their need, and every desire they had was satisfied as the land they owned was filled with gold, pearls, and onyx. They lived in the garden called Eden, which meant "pleasure and delight," and it was filled with every imaginable fruit for their enjoyment. There were no weeds in their fields nor blight on their fruit trees and roses. Mrs. Adam was heralded as the woman who had everything.

Every evening she and her husband attended this continual party with God in the garden. They loved listening to His words, and they ran to Him with shameless abandonment whenever they heard the sound of His arrival. The Lord loved her and her husband and enjoyed His time with them. He gave them everything He had created because He so greatly cherished them. He even told them to eat from the tree of life, which gave them immortality.

Only one tree did God ask them not to eat from, the tree of knowledge of good and evil, because with that knowledge came the painful understanding of the difference between blessing and calamity. Only this one thing was withheld from them, but even that was because of His great desire to protect them from pain. But Mrs. Adam became curious.

Imagine with me how it might have happened:

One morning, Mrs. Adam asked, "Why is this tree of knowledge of good and evil bad for us?"

"I don't know why it's not good for us, but we are to simply trust Him," Mr. Adam explained.

"I don't even understand what it means not to trust Him. Help me to understand, lest I accidentally do the very thing I shouldn't do," she pleaded.

"Just stay away from the tree. To trust God means to obey Him. He has given us unlimited freedom to enjoy all that our eyes can see. The only thing He has asked of us is that we don't eat fruit from that one tree. Once we eat of it, we will understand what evil is. I do know that evil is everything that God is not."

"That's it?" Mrs. Adam responded with surprise. "All that my eyes behold is ours? Everything is ours except that one tree? What more could we possibly want than what we see here in our own home?" So Mrs. Adam was content with all that the Lord had given to her—at least for a while longer.

Life or death, blessings or calamity had been laid before her. The power of choice was hers. She could choose to enjoy all that pleased her loving God, or she could choose to experience everything that He cast away from His presence. She could choose to taste of fruit that nourished her life, or to swallow garbage that would drain the very essence of her womanhood.

What would you have done?

What if we had been the first woman to be tempted to do the wrong thing? How long would we have resisted the fruit of the tree of knowledge of good and evil? How long would we have lasted in the Garden of Eden? Perhaps the more important question for us would be: *How long did we last before we forfeited the innocence of our childhood for the knowledge of evil?*

It doesn't matter if we were the first woman on earth or the one-billionth woman to face the choice of blessing or calamity. Adam failed the test, and every man who was born after him failed to choose life. Following him, we have all failed the test. We have all used the liberty of our free will to choose curses instead of God's blessing in our lives.

> All have sinned and are falling short of the honor and glory which God bestows and receives.
>
> ROMANS 3:23 AMP

Yes, Mrs. Adam, the woman who had everything that was good, wanted more. But if all we have had is good, the only thing we haven't had is the experiential grief of having nothing. That is what our enemy, Satan, the devil, wants for all of mankind. He wants to take away our blessings because he knows that the only way he can hurt God is to hurt God's children. He's in a war against God, and the battle is over our souls. His only weapon against us is his ability to deceive us through twisting the truth.

Satan, this vile serpent, came to Mrs. Adam and planted doubt in her heart against her Creator saying,

> "Isn't it true that God said you could not eat of every tree in the garden?"
>
> "We may eat of all the trees except the one called 'The Knowledge of Good and Evil.' We aren't to touch that one or we will die." But God had not told them not to *touch* it. He told them not to *eat* of it.
>
> Satan used her own misunderstanding against her. "You won't die," he said confidently, knowing that touching it would not destroy her, but that eating it would. He continued, "Go ahead, touch it and see if what I say is true. Not only that," he added, "if you eat of it, you will be like God, who knows the difference between good and evil."
>
> So Mrs. Adam touched the fruit that had tempted her and discovered that she did not die. She then doubted the instruction the Lord had given her. Holding the fruit in her hand, she examined this forbidden mystery. She concluded it would be good to be like God, whose friendship she enjoyed each evening. So she took the fruit to Mr. Adam, and they explored together the one thing God said they should not have.

Some philosophers defend Eve's fall into sin as a sincere drive to know God better. The Word teaches clearly that she was *deceived* by Satan. Perhaps she believed she would think more like the Father whom they loved if she knew the difference between good and evil.

God's Word does not say that Adam was deceived. It says that he heeded the voice of his wife, implying that with full knowledge of the consequences, he made a decision to do something against God's instruction. Here we see an illustration of the great influence a wife has over her husband. He listened to her and knowingly chose disobedience to God in order to be with her.

Can you see the great war that the enemy has waged over the woman? He could not have worked through the woman in this way unless a high value had been placed on her both by her lover and her Lord. He knew the influence she had over her husband. He knew the passion that both her lover and her Lord felt for her. But he did not foresee the great lengths to which her Lord would go to win her back.

As the bitterness of the fruit dripped onto their lips, both Adam and Eve were filled with panic. In that millisecond of deception and disobedience they instantly knew the horror of regret, the despair of remorse, and the loneliness of feeling separated from all the goodness of God. That one act of tasting forbidden fruit caused them to be suddenly alienated from one another, from the one who had moments before been so much a part of their own flesh that they were known by the same name.

They wanted to hide, and so they did.

Why are you hiding?

After they had eaten the fruit of the tree that God had told them to resist, they heard God walking in the garden and hid in the trees. It was time for the party, but the guests of honor refused to come.

God called to Adam, which is what He called both of them in those days, and He said, "Where are you?"

But they would not answer Him.

Have you ever been shopping with a small child in a department store who hid herself in the racks of clothes and would not reveal herself to you? There is nothing more heartrending than seeing a mother who cannot find her child in a large public place. She knows the possibilities are endless as to where her child may have gone.

An unbearable grief instantly grips the mother's heart as she considers that something may have happened that will keep her from ever seeing her child again. She calls with compassion and panic, "Where are you? Please come to me from wherever you are!" Everyone in the store rallies to help her find the lost child and restore her to her loving mother. And everyone cheers when the child is once again in her mother's arms.

God cried out to Adam and Eve with the same compassion that a mother has for her lost child. Yes, He knew where they were, and He knew that they had done something that would make them want to keep hiding from Him for the rest of their lives. That must have grieved Him more than we can comprehend. He knew that if Adam and Eve couldn't stand before Him without shame, they would never enjoy the true delight of His love which He intended for them to receive.

Please follow my paraphrased version of Genesis, chapter 3:8–24, recalling the painful conversation they had, and consider if this is a conversation that you might have had with God if you had done the one thing He had told you not to do.

God called out to His children, "Where are you, Adam?"

Adam responded, "I am afraid of You because I am ashamed."

God asked him, "Who told you to be ashamed?"

But Adam dropped his eyes and looked away from his Father.

"Have you done the one thing which I commanded you not to do?" God asked him, hoping that he would admit his mistake.

But Adam couldn't confess the truth, so he said, "The woman You gave to me gave me the fruit that I ate."

And Eve couldn't confess her mistake, for she said, "The serpent tricked me into eating the fruit."

I wonder what would have happened if they had admitted their wrongdoing? What if they had confessed their secret sin? Would the horrid consequences of their wrongdoing have been changed? What if Adam and Eve had known to trust God's unconditional love for them and had honestly admitted they had been disobedient?

God knew that if they could see how much He loved them, they would not be afraid to tell Him the truth, so He initiated His great plan of redemptive love for Adam, for Eve, and for us all.

Do you know how much God loves you?

After telling Adam and Eve what the consequences of their choice to do evil would bring into their lives, God demonstrated

His love for them by making garments to cover their naked-ness so they would come out of their hiding places. He covered their shame with the skins of an animal, thus illustrating the first death and sacrifice of life to pay for the wages of sin. This was a foreshadowing of Jesus' death, the final Lamb who was sacrificed for our sins.

> For the wages of sin is death, but the gift of God is eternal life in Jesus Christ our Lord.
>
> ROMANS 6:23

Knowing that underneath their new clothes, they still felt ashamed of themselves, God sent them away from the Tree of Life, lest they would eat of it and live forever in their broken relationship with Him. (See Genesis 3:22–23.) God put them out of Eden because He loved them. It is difficult to comprehend, but keeping them from the Tree of Life was an act of grace. He didn't want them to live forever with this guilt and shame on them. He separated them from the Tree of Life and immediately began His plan to win His children back.

Who told you to be ashamed?

God wasn't the one who told Adam and Eve to be ashamed. He didn't tell them not to come to the garden party. He was faithfully waiting for them. The invitation was still standing, even though He knew what they had done. It was their loss of innocence, their failure to trust Him, and their knowledge of evil that robbed them of their confidence to approach Him. Their secret sin, their rebellion against His instructions, had caused them to be ashamed of themselves. He wanted to restore them to the place where they would run with open arms to Him again.

It didn't matter to God who was first to sin. The one who was seduced and the one who knowingly submitted to seduction both suffered the shame of a secret that they didn't want to confess before God. Adam and Eve were both ashamed. It doesn't matter to God if you were the offender or the victim, the despair of sin is still the same, and God simply doesn't want you to live forever with that sense of shame separating you from His love.

God doesn't care about your secrets, He cares about your freedom to be honest with Him. He invites you to come out of hiding and into His arms, where He can restore the relationship of love and trust that He has always planned for you.

If you have secrets that make you want to hide from God, He wants you to confess those things to Him. In exchange for your confession, in exchange for believing that Jesus died so that you could live, in exchange for receiving His Holy Spirit to dwell inside of you, He will give you the power to be His child.

> But to as many as did receive and welcome Him, He gave the authority (power, privilege, right) to become the children of God, that is, to those who believe in (adhere to, trust in, and rely on) His name.
>
> JOHN 1:12 AMP

God invites us to accept His power to overcome the secrets in our lives. He will give us His overcoming power to fight off temptation. He invites us to draw near to Him when we are weak and afraid. Then He will fill us with His magnificent strength so we can triumphantly walk away from the bondage of our past and begin a new life in Him.

> For if anyone is a hearer of the word and not a doer, he is like a man observing his natural face in a mirror; for he observes himself, goes away, and immediately forgets what kind of man he was.
>
> JAMES 1:23–24 NKJV

CHAPTER
Three

Is That Any Way for a Princess to Act?

LIFE IS LIKE A FAIRY TALE!

Cinderella looked at the circumstances and believed that she was not worthy to receive what everyone else enjoyed. She couldn't imagine looking into the eyes of the Prince and feeling His admiration for her. Do you look forward to seeing the face of the Lord?

In the story of Snow White, the evil queen wanted to be the most beautiful woman in the kingdom. But the lovely Princess Snow White, who did not desire to be counted as the fairest one in all the land, was given the honor because of her pure heart and gentle ways.

A princess doesn't need to go to the mirror and ask, "Who's the fairest of us all?" She understands that her worth is defended by all the soldiers in her father's kingdom. She doesn't need to feel like she is the most beautiful or the most talented in all the land. She knows her value is not based on her own performance but on who her father is. Her value is inherited and is unconditional. Although she can change what she does, nothing can change who she is—the precious daughter of the King.

A princess doesn't pretend to be greater than those who defend her, but she humbly uses her protected freedom to serve others who are less fortunate than herself. Beautiful is the princess whose eyes are on the needs of her subjects and not upon herself.

Are you looking into mirrors or out of windows?

When we are given the opportunity to start our lives over through salvation in Jesus Christ, we should take full advantage of what it means to be born again. Our new position in the kingdom of God is not conditional. It does not depend upon what we have done in the past or what we will do in the future. Our title is based on who we are in Christ. Second Corinthians 5:17 explains,

> Therefore, if anyone is in Christ, he is a new creation; the old has gone, the new has come!

As a new creation, we are no longer subject to the evil prince of this world, but to the King of Kings. This means we can ignore the degradation of the devil's lies and enjoy the uprightness of our royal inheritance. This means we can forget about how others see us and focus on how we see others. We exchange our self-gratifying mirrors for windows that allow us to see the needs of others the way Jesus did.

We know that Jesus did not look into mirrors and submit

to anxiety over His appearance. No, He looked out through the windows of compassion and saw each new day as an opportunity to lift someone, to heal someone, to lead someone back to a closer relationship with God, the Father.

Sometimes we forget that we are no longer paupers. We are God's servants who bring the Gospel, the Good News of Jesus Christ, to those around us. I remember a most significant day when I met a young woman who needed encouragement. I could not have encouraged her if I had never been where she had been, if I had never felt alone or had forgotten the way she was feeling that day. But it is also true that I could not have helped her if I had not learned to enjoy my position in the kingdom of the living God.

I realized how far the Lord had brought me by seeing myself in her eyes. Her need to know Him was great. I was blessed to be the one to introduce her to her Father, to her inheritance in Him, and to her new title of princess.

My Secret Keeper reminded me that there is only one mirror we should look into every day, and sometimes many times a day. That mirror is the Word of God:

> For if anyone is a hearer of the word and not a doer, he is like a man observing his natural face in a mirror;
> For he observes himself, goes away, and immediately forgets what kind of man he was.
>
> James 1:23–24 NKJV

There is a blessing that comes from being a doer of the Word. When we administer grace to others, we can see ourselves in their hungry faces. We remember what kind of woman we used to be. To be whole enough to minister to the needs of others is the goal of our Christian walk. Then we see that God has taken us from grace to grace and from glory to glory. I wrote a letter to my Lord, about the joy I felt while looking into a young woman's eyes and seeing the reflection of God's love for me by seeing His love for her.

Dear Secret Keeper,

This has got to be the most memorable altar call that I have ever experienced. There were souls kneeling, lying prostrate, and standing. But they were all crying out to You for deliverance, forgiveness, and direction. And You were walking in and out of them, weaving a new pattern for their lives.

It was very difficult for me to maintain my composure, for I kept thinking about all that You had done for me. I thought about how You had called me holy when I had felt most undeserving. The sound of their lamentations was superseded only by the whisper of Your voice in my ear, rehearsing Your love for us.

Through swollen, tear-filled eyes I surveyed the crowd. There were as many men as there were women. Even teens and children raised their hands in surrender and submission to Your presence. For each individual there seemed to be an assigned angel of comfort. It was so awesome to see lives transformed by Your loving forgiveness.

Suddenly, I remembered when I had been at this place with You before. I didn't know You personally, but even then I knew that I could not live without You. I was desperate to know the power of Your forgiveness. I had felt that my life was in complete disarray. But I wondered how I could ask someone that I didn't have a relationship with to help me? I certainly did not want to

*use You to get out of my mess so that as soon as it was convenient
I could return to the way things had been before. I wanted change,
not as a temporary solution, but as a continued lifestyle. I was
just like these people for whom You were now leading me to pray.
I too had had to make You my Lord of all.*

*Now, through Your leading, I began to surge through the
crowd, exhorting the broken to rush into Your waiting arms. I
whispered in their ears, "You'll never be the same!" "I've sat where
you've sat!" Faces too numerable to commit to my memory passed
before me, each crying for a closer walk with You.*

*I felt weightless as I forged through the worshipers. Some were
being slain in the spirit and fell as I gently touched them. There
seemed to be a fog of glory; it was almost dreamlike. Then the
fog lifted and through the eyes of my heart, I could see only one
person.*

*There was a young lady standing in front of me. Surely, she
had not been there all along. How could I have laid hands on
everyone around her and not seen her? She stood there silently
with her head bowed, tears streaming down her face. Her arms
were folded just below her breast, resting on what I soon realized
was a promised birth.*

*Dressed neatly outwardly, I could discern that inwardly she
was in great turmoil. I approached her ever so tenderly, noticing
everything about her. Somehow I knew this was her first attempt to
approach You. I wanted to make the introduction. I took her left
hand away from the precious shelf it rested upon. Her hand was
ringless. You prompted me, and I knew that the bowed head was
not only a result of the guilt of sin but the shame of it as well.*

*"This is a wonderful day to give your life to the Lord," I
whispered in her ears. "He doesn't care what you've done; if you*

ask Him to forgive you, He will. He loves you, and He will never change His mind about you. You can depend on Him to always be there for you. Won't you give your heart to Him? He will mold you into the mother that you need to be."

With these words she raised very sorrowful eyes to mine, and we immediately traded places. In her eyes I saw myself. Through her eyes I saw You, Secret Keeper.

There are some failures and tragedies that we experience in life from which we feel we can never recover. It seems as if all of the exit ramps are closed and the detours endless. But when I get a glimpse of You, as I did in that moment of exchange with this young woman, I know that there is still help for the helpless.

I wanted with all of my strength to usher her into Your arms so that You could restore her fallen soul. I had felt Your arms before when I had despaired of life itself and had wondered if there was hope for me at all.

Somehow I wanted her to fully understand the words of my Secret Keeper from 2 Corinthians 5:17. If she is in Christ, she is a new creation! Her old life is gone, and her new life has come! This was not a temporary bandage for her pain. God was performing a miraculous change in her heart. *He* was making the changes; the work was not for her to do. She simply was to receive His grace and take a new look at the blessings He was putting into her new life.

I could not bring myself to look into her eyes and walk out of her heart without depositing hope in her spirit. Her new responsibility of motherhood did not mean that life was over for her. She still had years and years ahead of her if she allowed You to patch her together and heal her brokenness. I wanted to convince her to put not only her life but also her unborn child's life into Your hands. As she exchanged places with me, she saw how You could turn her shame to glory through Your simple plan of salvation. In an instant, You unraveled the complexities of the issues in her life.

As I held her in my arms, You held us both and rocked away the pain. We both repeated after You the sinner's prayer. We both received forgiveness. We both felt shameless. Our past was behind us with the promise of a bright future. Through grateful eyes we stared at one another and only You knew the depth of the secret we shared.

The Lord reaffirmed what we felt in our hearts that day by bringing this scripture to my mind as I wrote to Him.

For with the heart man believeth unto righteousness; and with the mouth confession is made unto salvation.

For the scripture saith, Whosoever believeth on him shall not be ashamed.

Romans 10:10–11 KJV

We believed on the Lord and our shame was lifted. I continued:

All we really need is You, Secret Keeper. You know all of our tormented secrets and the shame that tries to consume us. Yet You teach us to share each testimony for Your glory. Thank You for not allowing us to be swallowed up in guilt. I know Your power and will tell of it to others. It is because of Your mercies

that we are not consumed, because Your compassions fail not. (See
Lamentations 3:22.)

    Love,

    Serita Ann

To be whole enough to minister to the needs of others is the goal of our Christian walk. Then we see that God has taken us from grace to grace and from glory to glory.

I have looked into mirrors and out through windows, and I have found that it is better to look for windows of opportunity to help others than to grasp for glimpses of my own reflection. I have been on both sides of an altar. I have knelt there because I needed help, and I have knelt beside those who have needed encouragement. I understand now why it is better to give than to receive, just as it is better to be a princess for God instead of His pauper.

To be in a position to give, we must keep our hearts full of encouragement. The apostle Paul taught us in Ephesians 5:18–20 to be filled with the Holy Spirit. He says we can do that by speaking to one another with psalms, hymns, and spiritual songs. We should sing and make music in our heart to the Lord, always giving thanks to God the Father for everything, in the name of our Lord Jesus Christ.

Praying in tongues, as taught in 1 Corinthians 14:4, also keeps us built up. If we take responsibility to keep ourselves edified, we will not face the day like a pauper in search of provision. Our heart will be filled with intercession, ready to meet the demands of our Father's kingdom, and we will act like princesses ready to distribute the good news of our Father's provision.

If our hearts are continually full of praise to God, we will be prepared to serve in a moment's notice. We will be ready to say yes when our Master calls us. Our knees will already be bent on the side of the altar that gives instead of being there to receive.

Esther was a wonderful example of a woman who looked through windows of opportunity to help others. When the Lord summoned her to service, she was ready to respond to the work her Lord had prepared for her. We've all been summoned into the presence of the Lord. Will we be ready to say, "I will do as You ask, Lord," as Esther did? We will look more fully at the impact of Esther's willingness to submit to God's call in the next chapter, but first we will study together the illustration of a woman whose beauty soured when her focus was on herself instead of on the needs of her lord.

The story begins in the first chapter of Esther, verse 10. It's a long passage, but I want you to see the whole story.

> On the seventh day, when King Xerxes was in high spirits from wine, he commanded the seven eunuchs who served him—Mehuman, Biztha, Harbona, Bigtha, Abagtha, Zethar and Carcas—to bring before him Queen Vashti, wearing her royal crown, in order to display her beauty to the people and nobles, for she was lovely to look at.
>
> But when the attendants delivered the king's command, Queen Vashti refused to come. Then the king became furious and burned with anger.

Since it was customary for the king to consult experts in matters of law and justice, he spoke with the wise men who understood the times and were closest to the king—Carshena, Shethar, Admatha, Tarshish, Meres, Marsena and Memucan, the seven nobles of Persia and Media who had special access to the king and were highest in the kingdom.

"According to law, what must be done to Queen Vashti?" he asked. "She has not obeyed the command of King Xerxes that the eunuchs have taken to her."

Then Memucan replied in the presence of the king and the nobles, "Queen Vashti has done wrong, not only against the king but also against all the nobles and the peoples of all the provinces of King Xerxes.

"For the queen's conduct will become known to all the women, and so they will despise their husbands and say, 'King Xerxes commanded Queen Vashti to be brought before him, but she would not come.'

"This very day the Persian and Median women of the nobility who have heard about the queen's conduct will respond to all the king's nobles in the same way. There will be no end of disrespect and discord.

"Therefore, if it pleases the king, let him issue a royal decree and let it be written in the laws of Persia and Media, which cannot be repealed, that Vashti is never again to enter the presence of King Xerxes. Also let the king give her royal position to someone else who is better than she.

"Then when the king's edict is proclaimed throughout all his vast realm, all the women will respect their husbands, from the least to the greatest."

The king and his nobles were pleased with this advice, so the king did as Memucan proposed.

He sent dispatches to all parts of the kingdom, to each province in its own script and to each people in its own language, proclaiming in each people's tongue that every man should be ruler over his own household.

ESTHER 1:10–22

This is a fascinating account of two women. One spent much time looking into mirrors and was so taken by her own beauty that she forgot the benefits that come from bringing pleasure to others. The other was more beautiful than the first, but she was more interested in the needs of her people than in her own prosperity. The first had the title of queen, but the latter acted like one. Which one do you suppose held the title the longest?

The king had asked Vashti, the queen, to show the people and the princes her beauty, for she was fair to look on. But when Queen Vashti refused to come at his command, the king's anger burned in him. Imagine the event. Vashti was invited to a royal banquet where everybody who was anybody was there. Everybody whom the king wanted to impress was there. Everybody who was impressed by the king was there. They were having a wonderful, political celebration.

The king was upon his throne and servants were all around him. They were eating and making merry, and the queen, Vashti, was in another part of the palace entertaining her feminine court. Everybody knew Xerxes and Vashti. They were the crème de la crème of the kingdom. Everybody wanted to be like them when they grew up. And right in the middle of the celebration the king stood up and sent his servants scurrying, saying to them, "I command Vashti to come into the presence of her king." He probably sat down with great expectancy.

When the servants went into Vashti's chambers, they most likely found the women giggling, acting silly, and talking about their children and their husbands. They were celebrating being the queen's guests. The servants said, "Queen Vashti, King Xerxes commands your presence."

Queen Vashti looked into the eyes of the servant in the midst of her court royal, and said, "No."

The queen told the king no?

The wife told her husband who had commanded her to come, no?

Now, I'm a little confused here. I know this is not a book about marriage, but if my "king" called me right now, I would be "outta here"! I would turn off the computer and put my ministry of writing aside. I don't understand what Vashti was thinking, but since I'm not teaching on marriage right now, maybe I'll address that in my next book.

We're looking at the spiritual parallel in this story. But she did not act like a princess that day. She acted like a spoiled, vain woman who thought only of herself. The king called the queen and she refused to appear before him. Now, theologically, I'm not here to debate what the king's motives were, because it doesn't matter what he wanted. What matters is that he called her.

He called her just as the Lord has called us. Have we ever refused the King of Kings when He has summoned us into the presence of God? The Lord has called us over and over and over and yet haven't we told Him no?

Vashti's downfall is only a small part of this story:

Later when the anger of King Xerxes had subsided, he remembered Vashti and what she had done and what he had decreed about her.

Then the king's personal attendants proposed, "Let a search be made for beautiful young virgins for the king.

"Let the king appoint commissioners in every province of his realm to bring all these beautiful girls into the harem at the citadel of Susa. Let them be placed under the care of Hegai, the king's eunuch, who is in charge of the women; and let beauty treatments be given to them.

"Then let the girl who pleases the king be queen instead of Vashti." This advice appealed to the king, and he followed it.

Now there was in the citadel of Susa a Jew of the tribe of Benjamin, named Mordecai son of Jair, the son of Shimei, the son of Kish,

Who had been carried into exile from Jerusalem by Nebuchadnezzar king of Babylon, among those taken captive with Jehoiachin king of Judah.

Mordecai had a cousin named Hadassah, whom he had brought up because she had neither father nor mother. This girl, who was also known as Esther, was lovely in form and features, and Mordecai had taken her as his own daughter when her father and mother died.

When the king's order and edict had been proclaimed, many girls were brought to the citadel of Susa and put under the care of Hegai. Esther also was taken to the king's palace and entrusted to Hegai, who had charge of the harem.

The girl pleased him and won his favor. Immediately he provided her with her beauty treatments and special food. He assigned to her seven maids selected from the king's palace and moved her and her maids into the best place in the harem.

ESTHER 2:1–9

When Vashti said no, the king found someone who would say yes. Like King Xerxes, God always has somebody else He can call. God will not be left without a witness. If we won't allow Him to bless us so that our testimony can win multitudes of people, then He will find someone else upon whom to bestow His kindness. God can always find somebody who would like a chance to move from rags to riches, who needs a miracle to become a princess. He will find her even if she is under a bridge or in a homeless shelter. God will find somebody who will say, "I will, I will! I will let You make me into a princess, and I will respond to Your call!"

Oh, but the Father wants all of us to reflect His glory. He wants all of us to dress in the wedding garment He has designed for us. Does it matter that He only wants to stand us before His enemy and say, "Look at my beautiful daughter"? Does it matter that He wants so little from us? Will we respond to the task He wants us to do? Oh, that we might respond like Esther did. She said, "Here am I, Lord. Send me. I'll go."

Conditions might not be right when He calls us. We might be dirty. We might be lost in sin, not knowing the way out. But

He will call, and all we need to say is yes for Him to restore our souls.

Oh my Lord, my Secret Keeper, I pray that You ask my sister who is reading this book to come into Your presence, now that she knows all she needs to do is say, "Yes, Lord, I will come."

We were therefore buried with him through baptism into death in order that, just as Christ was raised from the dead through the glory of the Father, we too may live a new life.

ROMANS 6:4

CHAPTER
Four

Wash Off Those Cinders!

LIFE IS LIKE A FAIRY TALE!

*When Cinderella's fairy godmother told her the good news
that she could go to the ball, Cindy washed off the ashes
of her despair and left her own little corner in her own
little room. Haven't you heard the Good News?
Your Father God has rescued you.*

God does not expect us to be in perfect condition before we say yes to His offer to rescue us. He simply wants His daughters to come forward, to step out of the shadows and into His light, where He can stand us before all those who look toward Him and say, "Look at My daughter. Look how beautiful she is. Behold her countenance of peace and her fine garments that I have put upon her. Surely, whoever looks at her can see that she has a Father who loves and cares for her."

In our willingness to let God's grace rest upon us and stand as a testimony to His good works, we become the testimony of His power. He did not ask for workers, He asked for witnesses.

He did not ask us to perform, but to tell of His wondrous performance, the loving things we have seen Him do for us and for others.

God offers to each of us what was offered to Esther. The king's servants looked everywhere for a replacement for Vashti, the woman who had said no. They looked in the top parts of the city, where the upper echelon of the community lived. They gathered women from the homeless shelters. They went into the colleges and universities.

They invited the women who had been appointed as the least likely to succeed and gave them an opportunity to apply for the role of queen. Where did God's servants have to look to find us? Do we remember? Where were we when the Holy Ghost arrested us? Did He walk right into the club, right into that business meeting, and say, "The king has need of thee"?

It doesn't matter where we were. It matters that we were ready to say, "Yes, Lord. I will be the princess who offers testimony of Your grace. Choose me." It only matters that we were willing to come out of our corner to see what the Lord had ready for us.

The Scriptures are full of people like you and me. Abraham, the pagan Gentile, became the father of many nations. Joseph, the boy who was sold into bondage by his brothers, became the prime minister of Egypt. David, the shepherd boy, became the king of Israel. And our queen today, Esther the orphan, became the queen of King Xerxes. Just like a fairy tale, these people were taken from low and humble beginnings and lifted up to places of honor where they could serve and protect multitudes of God's people.

Each of them, however, had to leave behind their old lifestyles in order to accept the new blessings God had for them.

Esther was ready to say yes to God's call on her life. King Xerxes was only asking her to be a wife. But in that simple act of loving submission, she saved God's remnant and the precursors to the line of Jesus Christ from mass murder. Dreams do come true, and real people have lives that are better than fairy tales when they trust their decisions to God.

Something quite wonderful happened to Esther when she went to the king's palace. But first let's review the results of Queen Vashti's selfish reign. After Vashti said no to the king, he enforced a law for all women to respect and honor their husbands.

Reverence that was once motivated by love had become a requirement by law. The heart was no longer invited to be a part of the act. Husbands could no longer discern if their wives truly loved and respected them or if they were simply subject to a law in the land. Their wives did everything they were told, but were they acting out of love? To disobey their husbands was now punishable by a decree of the king. Could Vashti have ever dreamed that her own selfish actions would destroy the intimate partnerships of every couple in their kingdom?

When the wrath of King Xerxes was appeased, his servants ministered to him, "Let there be fair young virgins sought for the king. And let the maiden which pleaseth the king be queen instead of Vashti." (See Esther 2:1–2.)

So when the king's commandment was heard, many maidens were gathered together unto the custody of Hegai, keeper of the women. Esther was also brought to the king's house and put in the custody of Hegai. Esther pleased him and obtained his favor and kindness, so he speedily gave her things for purification. (See Esther 2:3–4, 8–9.)

His ways are better than fairy tales

I find this fascinating. Esther only needed to respond with a yes, and once she was in the king's palace, everything she needed for purification was given to her. She didn't have to shop first or buy fine dresses and perfumes in order to make herself beautiful for the king. He provided all she needed to look radiant, just as Jesus provides what we need to be purified. Hebrews 1:3 confirms this for us,

> The Son is the radiance of God's glory and the exact representation of his being, sustaining all things by his powerful word. After he had provided purification for sins, he sat down at the right hand of the Majesty in heaven.

If you have not understood this before, I hope that you comprehend what Good News this is for all of us. By believing in Jesus Christ, all the cinders of our past are washed away and we are purified, just as new babies are pure.

We celebrate this cleansing through water baptism as an outward testimony of what we know God has done to our secret soul. Jesus' blood redeems us from the penalty of our sins. The water of baptism celebrates the washing away of our habit of sin. Although we are saved by Jesus' blood, and not by being baptized, we are commanded by the Lord to submit to the act of baptism in the name of the Lord Jesus Christ.

If you have not followed the Lord in this act of obedience, I implore you to submit yourself to this wonderful ceremony He has prepared for you. Peter taught in Acts 2:38 that we are to repent and be baptized in the name of Jesus Christ for the remission of sins. He promised that we would receive the gift of the Holy Spirit. In Acts 10:47–48 we see that even those who had already received the Holy Spirit were commanded to be baptized in the name of the Lord.

There is a power that comes upon those who submit themselves to this public testimony that they accept God's gift of salvation. Through baptism we identify our past with His death, proclaiming that we are released from the bondage of sin.

Romans 6:1–8 explains what happens to us through baptism.

> What shall we say, then? Shall we go on sinning so that grace may increase?
>
> By no means! We died to sin; how can we live in it any longer?
>
> Or don't you know that all of us who were baptized into Christ Jesus were baptized into his death?
>
> We were therefore buried with him through baptism into death in order that, just as Christ was raised from the dead through the glory of the Father, we too may live a new life.
>
> If we have been united with him like this in his death, we will certainly also be united with him in his resurrection.
>
> For we know that our old self was crucified with him so that the body of sin might be done away with, that we should no longer be slaves to sin—
>
> Because anyone who has died has been freed from sin.

Now if we died with Christ, we believe that we will also live with him.

Water baptism marks the fact that we are separated from our past sins. Clean! Free from our indebtedness to the memory of wrongdoing! Water baptism is not simply a ritual that God asks us to do as a test of obedience. There is an authority with baptism that declares our independence from the powers that held us in bondage to our old nature.

When Jesus submitted to baptism, we know He did it to fulfill all righteousness. We also know that the Holy Spirit came upon Him in a visible way after He submitted Himself to baptism. His public ministry began after this testimony of His submission to God. We know that God announced His Sonship before the crowd during that public immersion. He was baptized so that His followers would do as He did. Matthew records that Jesus said,

> Whosoever therefore shall confess me before men, him will I confess also before my Father which is in heaven.
>
> MATTHEW 10:32 KJV

I have a friend who was baptized three times. Knowing I was working on this chapter, she shared her experience with me through the following letter,

Dear Lady Jakes,

I was first baptized when I was eight years old. I remember that my pastor asked me if I wanted to repent of my sins, and I said yes. I had loved God since I was four years old.

No one had yet told me about Jesus. No one in the church had explained to me that Jesus paid the price for my sins and the baptism was to celebrate the truth of this cleansing from my old nature. No one told me that Jesus was God, or that He wanted to be my personal friend.

Then we changed churches to another denomination, and I had to be baptized again in order to become a member of the church. So at eleven years old I was baptized a second time.

Finally, when I was twelve someone explained to me salvation through Jesus Christ. It was then that I finally understood that I would not go to heaven because I went to church, but because He had paid the price through the shedding of His blood for all the sins that separated me from God.

When I was seventeen a zealous young minister asked me if I had been baptized since I believed in the Lord Jesus. I couldn't believe that God would ask me to be baptized a third time. "Doesn't He know I love Him by now?" I questioned.

But one night I read the account of believers in Acts 19 who had been baptized by John unto repentance and were told to be baptized again now that they had received Jesus. Their story was just like mine.

The third time I was baptized, only the minister was present beside me, but I felt like all of heaven and hell were watching me. It took great humility to do it again, but I didn't want to miss any blessing that my Father might have for me. When I came up out of the water that third time, the minister told me to expect to receive the gift of tongues just as believers in Acts 19 had experienced. He told me to say whatever words came to mind and not to worry if they sounded strange.

I could only whisper "Abba," not knowing at that young age that it meant Father and was the same word Jesus used to cry unto His Father.

Needless to say, that day of my third baptism marked the beginning of my ministry. There was no turning back for me after that powerful day of testimony before my cloud of witnesses. I have remained in full-time ministry now for thirty years. It truly was the day that the Holy Spirit came upon me with the power to be a witness for Him.

I hope my letter will encourage your readers to find the cleansing power of His baptismal waters, now that they believe in Christ alone.

Love,
Your Sister in the Lord

Dreams do come true, and real people have lives that are better than fairy tales when they trust their decisions to God.

This sister's experience well illustrates the power of water baptism. There are many scriptures that explain the grace that comes upon us during this important event with God. The apostle Paul wrote,

> For you did not receive a spirit that makes you a slave again to fear, but you received the Spirit of sonship. And by him we cry, "Abba, Father."

> ROMANS 8:15

For this precious woman, it was as though baptism confirmed her adoption. She was given His name to call upon before anyone ever told her that her Daddy's name was Abba. Galatians 4:6 shows that the Spirit of Jesus, the Holy Spirit, is the one who told her who sealed her adoption by giving her the name that she was now to use. The scripture reads,

> Because you are sons, God sent the Spirit of his Son into our hearts, the Spirit who calls out, "Abba, Father."
>
> GALATIANS 4:6

Read the rest of this passage to see the good news that is in store for us.

> So you are no longer a slave, but a son; and since you are a son, God has made you also an heir.
> Formerly, when you did not know God, you were slaves to those who by nature are not gods.
> But now that you know God—or rather are known by God—how is it that you are turning back to those weak and miserable principles? Do you wish to be enslaved by them all over again?
>
> GALATIANS 4:7–9

No, God does not leave us to fend for ourselves against our old ways. He gives us the power to be His daughters. Acts 1:8 declares,

> But you will receive power when the Holy Spirit comes on you; and you will be my witnesses in Jerusalem, and in all Judea and Samaria, and to the ends of the earth.

What a wonderful God we serve! Not only does He do all the work to save us, He does all the work to cleanse us. All we need to do is walk into His water and let Him wash away the cinders of our past life. Our old nature remains buried as we rise up to walk in newness of life.

Queen Esther enjoyed her new life as first lady in the king's house. She served with such humility that the king favored her above all others. She didn't go before the king with excuses as to why she couldn't be his queen. She didn't use the excuses we hear in the Church like, "Well, you don't know my mamma, and my daddy, and then my children, and I've got a husband in jail and. . . ."

Nor did Esther do what I did to the Bishop when he asked me to be his lady. I told him, "I don't play, I don't sing, and I can't preach." All he said to me was, "But what *can* you do?"

Don't go to God telling Him who you're not! He knows us. He knows everything about us and He called us anyway. Don't give God a negative résumé. Instead, tell Him, "I can do all things through Christ who strengthens me." (See Philippians 4:13.)

The Bible says that Esther obtained kindness and favor. She still had to go through the same thing everybody else went through, but it was easier for her because she already had favor. We have favor through the grace of God. Grace is the unmerited favor and power of God on our lives as taught in 2 Corinthians 12:9:

> But he said to me, "My grace is sufficient for you, for my power is made perfect in weakness." Therefore I will boast all the more gladly about my weaknesses, so that Christ's power may rest on me.

Now just because we have favor with God does not mean we are going to escape going through our "go-throughs." We're not exempt from difficulty. He loves us, and He will walk us through it, but through it we all must go. Some of us will go through the water, some of us will go through the flood, and some of us through the fire.

I have favor, but it doesn't keep me from going through things. The one sustaining force that has never changed is the knowledge that the King has called me. Moreover, because I found favor with the King, He's with me every step of the way, just as He is with you.

Favor. You must remember that it is undeserved. You can't earn God's grace so you can't lose it. His unmerited favor is a free gift that comes to us with our salvation. Simply enjoy His provision and prepare yourself to please and serve Him.

Favor changes the way things are going

Esther's turn came after all the women were paraded before the king, both the haves and the have-nots. Everybody came before the king for him to find a suitable queen. Then his eyes saw Esther. The king favored her above every other woman who was in the room.

Aren't those secret moments with God, when we feel like we are His favorite, wonderful? It is okay to admit that we have felt that way, because He makes us all feel singled out and loved. Sometimes, don't we feel like we are above all the other people in the world, because He chose us? Out of all the people that He could have selected, somehow in His infinite wisdom, He saw what we would become, not what we used to be, but what we are going to be, and He favored us. He did us a favor. Esther must have felt that way the day she stood before the king.

Customarily, after all of the virgins had paraded before the king, there were three places to which they could be assigned. The first chamber was reserved for all whom the king had basically sent on their way because he didn't want to become further involved with them.

The second chamber was where those women whom he liked a little bit were sent. The Bible calls them concubines. He entered into a pseudo relationship with them, without a covenant. Today we call them "live-ins."

The third chamber was reserved for the queen. Those three places reveal three ways that we can approach God. We can be satisfied just to have a mundane Sunday morning experience with Him, which would be the first chamber. Everybody can do that, and most of us do only that.

Then there is the second chamber, where we get just close enough to the glory to brush up against it and know that it's real. The problem is, we go no further and we want to be on a live-in basis so we can leave if things get inconvenient. To be a live-in with God is to say we don't trust Him to be "a rewarder of those who diligently seek Him." (See Hebrews 11:6.)

But there is a place reserved for intimacy, for those who have entered into a covenant relationship with God. This place is reserved for the queen, where we become intimate with Him, where we become wrapped up, tied up, and tangled up with Him, and we can't let Him go. It's a place where, once we have been there, we will never be satisfied to be anywhere else because we have been in the awesome presence of God.

That's where they put Esther—right into the queen's

chamber. They didn't even bother to return her to those other superficial, inner courts or outer courts. They took her right into the place where she could approach the king as her husband. This is where God wants us, the Holy of Holies where we can worship Him.

That's where I want to be—right in the presence of God! So day and night I can praise Him in the third chamber reserved for the queen. We are all to aspire to go into that third chamber, whether we are babes in Christ or mature, seasoned Christians. We've got ready access to the King of Kings. In the time of need, when nobody else is around, you know that your King is always present to carry you through whatever you have to go through. That's trust!

When the king saw Esther, he extended his scepter and said, "Whatever you want will be done, and I will give you up to half of my kingdom." Her story continues in Esther 7:2–10:

> And as they were drinking wine on that second day, the king again asked, "Queen Esther, what is your petition? It will be given you. What is your request? Even up to half the kingdom, it will be granted."
>
> Then Queen Esther answered, "If I have found favor with you, O king, and if it pleases your majesty, grant me my life—this is my petition. And spare my people—this is my request.
>
> For I and my people have been sold for destruction and slaughter and annihilation. If we had merely been sold as male and female slaves, I would have kept quiet, because no such distress would justify disturbing the king."

King Xerxes asked Queen Esther, "Who is he? Where is the man who has dared to do such a thing?"

Esther said, "The adversary and enemy is this vile Haman." Then Haman was terrified before the king and queen.

The king got up in a rage, left his wine and went out into the palace garden. But Haman, realizing that the king had already decided his fate, stayed behind to beg Queen Esther for his life.

Just as the king returned from the palace garden to the banquet hall, Haman was falling on the couch where Esther was reclining. The king exclaimed, "Will he even molest the queen while she is with me in the house?" As soon as the word left the king's mouth, they covered Haman's face.

Then Harbona, one of the eunuchs attending the king, said, "A gallows seventy-five feet high stands by Haman's house. He had it made for Mordecai, who spoke up to help the king." The king said, "Hang him on it!"

So they hanged Haman on the gallows he had prepared for Mordecai. Then the king's fury subsided.

Esther said yes to God's invitation to be a queen. Her willingness won His favor and in so doing she saved her people from genocide.

The scepter is in your hands

God is calling us something that we think we're not, but He knows us, who we really are. The scepter is now extended to us and He is saying, "Whatever you want, whatever you will, ask what you will and it shall be done unto you."

The scepter is extended toward you, so ask Him what you will. Let Him show you His love for you. Let Him prove His grace so that He might be glorified in the earth through the testimony of your praise. So reach out and grab hold of God's scepter, which is all that He has for you.

God just wants you to know that whatever you need from Him, He's able to provide. He has chosen you to be His daughter. He has provided the waters to make you pure. He has a plan to lift you up. All He wants is to hear you say to Him unequivocally, "Yes! Absolutely yes!"

> Now Joshua was dressed in filthy clothes as he stood before the angel. The angel said to those who were standing before him, "Take off his filthy clothes." Then he said to Joshua, "See, I have taken away your sin, and I will put rich garments on you."
>
> Zechariah 3:3–4

CHAPTER
Five

Put On a More Revealing Dress

LIFE IS LIKE A FAIRY TALE!

*Cinderella knew that if she wanted to dance with a prince,
she must dress like a princess. She willingly traded her rags
for the beautiful gown that had been made just for her.
Isn't it time you put on the garment of praise
to dance with the Lord?*

Cinderella was transformed simply by putting on the new dress that had been prepared for her. A new outfit can give us a sense of confidence over who we are, or at least over who we appear to be. Afternoon talk shows draw large audiences with promises of makeovers that change hard-looking women to beautiful cover girls. The ones who feel the makeover expresses who they really are inside smile radiantly as they come from behind the screens.

We all use clothes to cover our insecurities and boost our self-worth. Things haven't changed much since Adam and Eve first tried to hide behind fig leaves! God made clothes for them because the ones they made weren't very functional.

Many people will admit that even when they meet someone for the first time, they enjoy having on a new outfit to make that memorable first impression. They know that the person they are meeting wouldn't know whether their clothes were new or ten years old, but they still feel better through the nervousness of that first handshake when they are dressed in something fresh and stylish.

Most of us notice when a friend is wearing a new outfit that we have never seen on her before and agree that there is something satisfying to our own souls in seeing another woman look her best. Don't we all enjoy watching a well-dressed man or woman energetically enter a room with confidence? I'm not referring to the well-dressed people who enter a room and tacitly express, "Look at me." But we are charmed by immaculately groomed people who stand before us and imply, "Ah, there you are." What is this difference?

As wonderful as new clothes are, they do not make up for the grace of a humbled heart. First Peter 5:5–7 says,

> All of you, clothe yourselves with humility toward one another, because, "God opposes the proud but gives grace to the humble."
> Humble yourselves, therefore, under God's mighty hand, that he may lift you up in due time.
> Cast all your anxiety on him because he cares for you.

It's not easy to clothe ourselves in humility, but I have learned that the more we understand how very much God loves us, and the more we comprehend the grace He has demonstrated toward us, the more humble we become.

There is a false humility that cripples us, telling us we are not worthy of any good thing. This is humiliation and it is not from God. But godly humility affirms that all good things are ours only because of God's goodness and not our own. When we understand that God's love is unconditional, when we become aware that we can neither earn His love nor lose it, we are filled with awe toward Him, and it humbles us in His presence.

Applying this difference between humiliation and humility to our lives will clothe us more beautifully than the world's most fashionable clothiers and designers. A humbled heart does not ask for attention from others; it gives attention to others. Even this gift of humility comes to us from the Lord.

Secondhand Rose

We are all affected by seeing someone who needs a clean shirt, a mended hem, or a new pair of shoes, especially if they hang their head with embarrassment or humiliation. I well remember being the woman who needed something to wear to "the dance." I remember the insecurity of wondering whether or not others would feel I was acceptable. It wasn't so very long ago, though it now seems a lifetime away from where the Lord has carried me.

I pen these words as a testimony of what God can do. I want the words to encourage those who have given up on their future because of obstacles that seem to be immovable. Before I even began to write the following admission to my Secret Keeper, He reminded me of His desire to clothe me more beautifully than the lilies of the field, in garments of praise to His glory.

I remembered Zechariah's account of seeing Joshua, the high priest, standing before the angel of the Lord. Satan stood at his right side accusing him before God. Then the Lord said to Satan,

"The Lord rebuke you, Satan! The Lord, who has chosen Jerusalem, rebuke you! Is not this man a burning stick snatched from the fire?"

Now Joshua was dressed in filthy clothes as he stood before the angel.

The angel said to those who were standing before him, "Take off his filthy clothes."

Then he said to Joshua, "See, I have taken away your sin, and I will put rich garments on you."

ZECHARIAH 3:2–4

I wrote,

Dear Secret Keeper,

I was so excited as we prepared to attend our first National Convention as husband and wife. It was my first national appearance as my husband's new bride. I was so honored to be his helpmeet, and I wanted to represent him well.

As Pastor's wife, it seemed important to me that I looked the part of his "First Lady." I had such a hard time trying to pack my clothes. I certainly wanted to look my best; after all, I am the First Lady. I couldn't afford anything new, but I was so pleased with the suits, dresses, and shoes that the sisters from the church gave me out of their closets. They all fit almost perfectly. I didn't have enough things to change twice a day, but I knew I could wear the outfits from the beginning of the week again at the end of the week. I hoped no one would remember them.

I would be meeting so many prominent people. I prayed that I had selected my best pieces. When it was finally time to pack up the car and get on the road, I packed a lunch since it was a long drive to the conference. I felt the trip would be simply unforgettable.

But the Lord said to Samuel, "Do not consider his appearance or his height, for I have rejected him. The Lord does not look at the things man looks at. Man looks at the outward appearance, but the Lord looks at the heart."

1 SAMUEL 16:7

It was so embarrassing. Upon my arrival, everyone seemed to be staring, first at me, and then right through me. It was as though they were as embarrassed by me as I was for me. I tried so very hard to be appropriate.

I knew that this was a very special occasion for us. Everyone we thought was anybody had flown in for the occasion. But I didn't know that it was going to be so fashionable.

Suddenly, all of the things that the sisters from the church had given me seemed so dingy. The shoes turned over on my feet. And how could it be that the hem was always falling out of the dress I had chosen? If I could have found a corner in which to hide, I could have made it easier for them to ignore me; then I would have been just fine.

I wondered if You were as concerned about my appearance

as I was. And You answered my question as I entered the service. The anointing was so strong that many lay prostrate before You. The Word was so powerful that I soon forgot what I had on and who was around me. I began to think of all the wonderful things that You had done in my life and I began to weep.

I sensed Your presence reassuring me that You didn't care about what I had on, that Your mind was full of who I would become. I urgently rushed into Your presence and worshipped You. You changed my garments. Surely, I must have felt like Joshua when he stood in Your presence dressed in filthy garments. You must have instructed the angels to remove the filthy garments from me while You clothed me in righteousness.

To console those who mourn in Zion, to give them beauty for ashes, the oil of joy for mourning, the garment of praise for the spirit of heaviness; that they may be called trees of righteousness, the planting of the Lord, that He may be glorified.

ISAIAH 61:3 NKJV

That day seems so long ago and far away from me now. I can go into any store in any city or country and select the best, often without regard to price. The outward adornment is no longer from consignment stores, yet the inward self remembers how You attired me when I felt most naked.

You accepted me for who I was. You have given me favor and caused others to see what You saw. I will always depend on You to customize me to Your specificity. I trust You to mold and fashion me according to the pattern that You have chosen for my life.

I thought of the song that says, "I'm wearing hand-me-down

clothes, and that's why they call me Secondhand Rose." But You,
Secret Keeper, are fashioning me like the Rose of Sharon.
By the way, thank You for my new clothes.

Love,
Serita Ann

The Rose of Sharon

Just as the Lord covered the shame of Adam and Eve, He continues to replace our humiliation with humility. We are thankful that He is the one who clothes us. He covers us with His righteousness so that others see that we belong to Him. He is not ashamed of us, but He proudly covers us with His royal robe and stands us before our critics and accusers to boast, "She is mine."

As daughters of the living and only true God, it is time that we clothe ourselves with humility, revealing who we really are. When we enter a room, others should notice our countenance of peace instead of our dress. Our faces should shine with the oil of joy that results from knowing how much God loves us. Our words throughout the day should demonstrate a revelation of God's grace in our lives.

As the bride of Christ, we are each given a wedding gown, provided by Jesus, the Rose of Sharon, himself. He offers an exchange with us, our ashes for His beauty, our grief for His joy, our rags for His garment of praise. He eagerly extends this great exchange so that we will become like Him and glorify the Father by showing the world what a kind and awesome God we serve.

There have been many books on the market to teach us how

to dress for success. But the Lord tells us rather to clothe our-selves with Jesus Christ. What would happen if we, His daughters, consciously wrapped ourselves in His robe each morning as we prepared for the day?

What would this "putting on Christ" look like?

The apostle Paul explains how to do this in Colossians 3:12–17:

> Therefore, as God's chosen people, holy and dearly loved, clothe yourselves with compassion, kindness, humility, gentleness and patience.
>
> Bear with each other and forgive whatever griev-ances you may have against one another. Forgive as the Lord forgave you.
>
> And over all these virtues put on love, which binds them all together in perfect unity.
>
> Let the peace of Christ rule in your hearts, since as members of one body you were called to peace. And be thankful.
>
> Let the word of Christ dwell in you richly as you teach and admonish one another with all wisdom, and as you sing psalms, hymns and spiritual songs with gratitude in your hearts to God.
>
> And whatever you do, whether in word or deed, do it all in the name of the Lord Jesus, giving thanks to God the Father through him.

In Philippians 2:1–17, Paul further explains how we are to dress ourselves:

If you have any encouragement from being united with Christ, if any comfort from his love, if any fellowship with the Spirit, if any tenderness and compassion,

Then make my joy complete by being like-minded, having the same love, being one in spirit and purpose.

Do nothing out of selfish ambition or vain conceit, but in humility consider others better than yourselves.

Each of you should look not only to your own interests, but also to the interests of others.

Your attitude should be the same as that of Christ Jesus:

Who, being in very nature God, did not consider equality with God something to be grasped,

But made himself nothing, taking the very nature of a servant, being made in human likeness.

And being found in appearance as a man, he humbled himself and became obedient to death—even death on a cross!

Therefore God exalted him to the highest place and gave him the name that is above every name,

That at the name of Jesus every knee should bow, in heaven and on earth and under the earth,

And every tongue confess that Jesus Christ is Lord, to the glory of God the Father.

Therefore, my dear friends, as you have always obeyed—not only in my presence, but now much more in my absence—continue to work out your salvation with fear and trembling,

For it is God who works in you to will and to act according to his good purpose.

Do everything without complaining or arguing,

So that you may become blameless and pure, children of God without fault in a crooked and depraved generation, in which you shine like stars in the universe

As you hold out the word of life—in order that I may boast on the day of Christ that I did not run or labor for nothing.

But even if I am being poured out like a drink offering on the sacrifice and service coming from your faith, I am glad and rejoice with all of you.

Jesus looks at our hearts

Jesus comes to seek us out and save us. He comes looking for the real self who hides in corners and behind new clothes. We see Him searching for someone who is hiding when He went through Samaria on His way to Galilee. This particular route was not unusual from a geographical perspective. Going through Samaria was the shortest way. But Samaria was normally avoided by Jews.

For over 700 years, religious and racial prejudice had separated the Jews from the Samaritans, who were the descendants of the surviving Israelites from the northern kingdom and who intermarried with the newly imported Gentile population after the fall of Samaria in 722 BC. Samaritans worshipped God as the Jews did. They studied the five books of Moses (Genesis to Deuteronomy) but not the rest of the Old Testament. They awaited the coming of a prophet like Moses. But Jewish hatred for the

Samaritans sprang more from historical and racial considerations than from any fundamental difference of religion.[1]

However, Jesus was not like the other Jews. He decided that He must go through Samaria on this particular day. His beloved disciple John recorded the event in John 4:4, noting that Jesus had to go through Samaria. I like the way the *King James Version* states it, *And he must needs go through Samaria.* But *The Amplified Bible* says, *It was necessary for Him to go through Samaria.*

I believe it was *necessary* so Jesus could invite a certain woman at Jacob's well to be part of His family, which also illustrates His love for you and me. It was necessary for Jesus to meet this particular woman so that we could understand that His offer of salvation and hope is open to people even like us. Jesus wanted this Samaritan woman to know that she was included on His guest list. She was invited to drink from the rivers of living water He offers to everyone.

Jesus was tired from His journey, so He went to the well where this woman came for water. He knew she would come to the well at a time when the other women from the city would not be there. This woman didn't have a lot of money or she would have sent someone else to draw the water for her. She was "nameless" as far as the story goes, but she was most definitely a memorable woman. She didn't have a lot left to offer anyone—after all, she had already been used by several of the men in town.

Almost everyone in Samaria knew her, but they usually referred to her as "that woman." The tone in their voice and the sideways glance of their eyes clearly revealed they meant this

---

[1] *Eerdman's Handbook to the Bible,* David Alexander, Pat Alexander, Eds. (Grand Rapids: William B. Eerdmans Publishing Company, 1973), 497, 537.

woman whose name was not mentioned in nice family homes. No one ever walked up to her and said, "Hi, Zema." Instead, they would murmur under their breath when she passed them, "Hmmm, who is it this month? Who is it this year? What are you into now?"

Jesus comes to seek us out and save us. He comes looking for the real self who hides in corners and behind new clothes.

This woman's secrets alienated her from the women who came to the well together. No, this nameless woman had five secrets that had left her so devastated, she didn't even want to come to the well when the other women were there. Besides, she thought no one could relate to all that she had experienced.

Have you ever found it difficult to go to a ladies' meeting at church where other women don't know your name, but you think they know what you have done? Maybe you felt that no one else who went to those meetings had done what you had done. Maybe you could see that they were thirsty for some refreshment to quench their parched soul, but you could not see that their dryness was as severe as your own.

Who could you trust to know who you really are? Who would really understand the struggle it is for you to come into a room full of women whom you feel have it "all together." Surely those women at church who lead the ministries, who attend all the conferences, who drive nice cars, and who are not on welfare, wouldn't understand what you are going through. In one of my meetings, I once challenged a room filled with thousands of women to stand up if they had less than five things they didn't want somebody to know about them. No one stood, but they all applauded my discovery.

The Samaritan woman came to the well that eventful day and walked right into the very thing she had been running from. She walked head-on into Truth. She wanted to get something to drink because she was thirsty in more ways than one. A man was sitting at the well, and she had learned to be cautious of men who sat beside wells and found her alone. Such a scene reminded her of all of her past mistakes. Mistakes could have led to babies out of wedlock; mistakes could have led to rape; mistakes today could lead to new mistakes.

But on this day the man sitting at the well was waiting to let her know that she was not forgotten, and God had a new image for her to wear. Jesus let her know that He knew everything about her. He knew about the man she was living with who wasn't her husband. He knew about the husband she had had before him, and before him, and before him, and before him. He knew the emptiness that these relationships had left. He knew she was the one who thirsted for something to quench the dryness in her spirit. He knew He was the only one who could quench her thirst. He waited by the well for her.

When she came, He asked her for water. Surprised that a Jew would talk to a Samaritan, she asked Him how it was that He would ask her for water. "If you only knew the gift of God, if you knew who I am, you would ask Me to give you water, and I would give you living water so that you would never thirst again. The water that I would give you would become a spring of water welling up, flowing and bubbling continually within you unto eternal life." (See John 4:10–14.)

You're at the well, so drink!

Memories will never quench our thirst or put fresh, clean clothing on our souls. We need access to fresh water every day. We need to be loved every day. Memories are not enough to really satisfy us. If all we have to quench our thirst for love is from the memories of those five experiences in our past, or twenty-five, or one, or none, we will quickly dry up and die from our thirst. We need access to fresh, living water from a well that never runs dry. If parched, waterless memories hold us in bondage from our future, it's time to receive the gift of God.

The woman at the well sat down beside the Truth and was sanctified, clothed with righteousness, and set apart for special use in the kingdom of God. God didn't change her past to make her a messenger of Good News; He used her past to prove His unconditional love for her.

The woman at the well comes to our churches on Sundays. She comes to women's meetings. She reads this book. She doesn't need to be nameless anymore. The Father knows everything about her, wraps her in His robe of humility, and proudly calls her His own.

Jesus, the Incarnate Word of God, said to the woman at the well, "Give Me something to drink." The Word still says to us today, "Speak what you know to Me. Show Me how much of My Word you have hidden in your heart." Jesus still says to the woman who comes for water at the well, "Worship Me, say something to Me to let Me know that you want a relationship with Me. Say something to Me that will quench My thirst for you."

And the woman at the well says, "Why are You asking me

for something to drink? Shouldn't You have something with which to get Your own water?"

And the Lord says to the woman, "If you only knew who you were sitting with, it wouldn't matter what you have done. What would matter is that you are thirsty, and I can satisfy your thirst."

If you have never told the Lord that you are thirsty for Him, I implore you to stop reading this book and get alone with Him right now. Tell Him that you need Him to direct your life. Ask Him for that gift of God that He promised to the woman at the well. Your past is not worse than hers. Jesus purposely sought out the woman at the well to prove to you that He cares about your thirst too.

If you truly don't know how to talk to Jesus in your own words, then pray this prayer with me.

> *Lord, I am thirsty for Your living water. I confess that I am not proud of my past, but realize that I do not have the power to break away from the bondage of my memories without Your grace to set me free.*
>
> *I surrender my heart to You.*
>
> *I surrender my past to You.*
>
> *I thank You that my identity no longer aligns with who I have been but with who You are.*
>
> *I give You my future and choose not to be anxious about it anymore, knowing that You will lead me to green pastures and still waters where I will be cared for like a lamb with a loving shepherd.*
>
> *Thank You for filling me with Living Water that will keep me from thirsting again. Thank You for removing my filthy clothes and*

covering me in Your beautiful robe of humility and righteousness. Thank You for dressing me as a princess and revealing to others who I really am.

His divine power has given us everything we need for life and godliness through our knowledge of him who called us by his own glory and goodness.

2 PETER 1:3

CHAPTER
Six

Find Your Own Way to the Dance

LIFE IS LIKE A FAIRY TALE!

Cinderella's relatives wouldn't take her to the party with the family horses, so she took a taxi, better known in those days as a pumpkin pulled by mice. Where do you need to go? Whose permission are you waiting on? Have you checked the Yellow Pages for a ride?

Cinderella could have indulged herself in self-pity because her evil relatives had told her to stay home and refused her a ride to the ball. If she had waited for permission to do the right thing, she never would have married the prince. If she had stayed angry toward her evil sisters, she would not have enjoyed the party once she got there.

God lets us know right from wrong, and He gives us a way of escape from the evil that is plotted against us. He gives us the freedom to do the right thing. Hebrews 8:10–12 confirms this promise:

This is the covenant I will make with the house of Israel after that time, declares the Lord. I will put my laws in their minds and write them on their hearts. I will be their God, and they will be my people.

No longer will a man teach his neighbor, or a man his brother, saying, "Know the Lord," because they will all know me, from the least of them to the greatest.

For I will forgive their wickedness and will remember their sins no more.

God gives us permission to forget our past and the understanding to live our present. He said He will remember our sins no more! King David had many regrets. His past was full of sins and secrets, but look at what he discovered about God's love and recorded for each of us:

For as high as the heavens are above the earth, so great is his love for those who fear him; as far as the east is from the west, so far has he removed our transgressions from us.

PSALM 103:11–12

But there is still an enemy of God who wants to steal your freedom from you. The devil wants to keep you in the cinders of who you were to keep you from enjoying your inheritance. He loves to see you sitting in the corner, where you can become his easy prey. Not too long ago I nearly became the easy prey of the enemy. Without the comfort of my Secret Keeper and the prayers and love of my husband, family, and church family, I could have been trapped in the valley of the shadow of death.

Dear Secret Keeper,

When I received the phone call about my mother's condition, I knew I had to rush to her side. They had already put her in the intensive care unit. I was miles away at one of our conferences and would have to fly through the night to get home to her.

Early that next morning I drove to the hospital and, when I stepped out of the elevator, I looked into the eyes of a lady who had sat through the night outside the door of Mother's room. She looked so worried that my heart immediately began to sink. As she escorted me to the room where Mother was, there was a gloominess in the air.

When we arrived at the door, I felt the person I saw had to be another patient. I walked with horror past the bed to a window that had no view. My mother lay with IV poles all around her. An oxygen tube running to her nose insisted that she breathe. But the most devastating piece of hospital equipment in the room was the respirator, the life support system that sustained her life!

How did this happen? How did this happen to Mother? When did this happen? I struggled for my sanity as I stared into nothingness. This is my mother!

Oh, Secret Keeper, I could not find a prayer!

I backed toward the bed and stared into the face of one who had loved me all of my life. She slowly opened her eyes and stared at her baby.

"Mother, I didn't know. I'm here! Mother, I'm here." She couldn't speak at all. Only her eyes spoke of the terror in her heart.

For the first time in my life, I saw fear on Mother's half-masked face. She was so afraid. I had not been there to help her like she had helped me countless times.

Secret Keeper, I felt so guilty.

The nurse touched me on the shoulder and told me visiting hours were over. Over? I could only stay thirty minutes with the woman who had given me life?

In the waiting room, the doctors came to inform me of Mother's condition. It was Gillain-Barre, a rare disease that was as antiquated as polio in its derivation. It was a virus that resulted in paralysis from the neck down. The respirator was there because Mother's lungs were not functioning.

They shared with me that the virus was reversible barring any complications from an extended stay on the respirator. Let the fight begin! During the day, phone calls were made to my brothers and sisters. My husband left midway through the conference to join the vigil at the CCICU. Our extended family took shifts supporting us and staying through the night for updates on Mother's condition.

One night as I drove home, my spirit was so heavy. My tears mixed with the raindrops falling on my windshield to further obstruct my vision. I asked You a question, "Are You going to take her?"

I will never forget the sound of Your answer. You, my omniscient Passenger said, "Yes!" And I knew that You would do so. I wanted so much for You to say, "Not yet!" Or even, "Not now!" But I knew Your voice.

For the next day or two, visitor after visitor came to stand by Mother's bed and pray for her. I looked in their faces to see if they sensed the urgency that I felt over her condition and her expected end. They were most comforting in their presence and in their remarks. I think everyone loved her with the same hope of her recovery. But I remembered Your answer, Secret Keeper.

That morning that I arrived to go in to Mother, her kidneys had failed. Dialysis was their prescription. Fifteen minutes into the procedure, I heard a page for Mother's doctor to report to CCICU station! As though I were one of the doctors, I began to run toward her room. As I rounded the wall, I saw the response team pull her gown open and apply pressure to her heart.

Her heart had arrested and so had mine. I remembered Your answer and knew that You had come to take her. The nurse reassured me that they had a heartbeat. I inched toward her side to look into eyes that were set on You. They started the procedure again for someone who had already been stolen from her body. I went back to the waiting room only to hear the doctors being summoned again. No one came to notify the family this time.

Without their invitation, I went to the room that once housed Mother to face a nurse whose nod from side to side affirmed what I already knew—she was gone with You, Secret Keeper. She received her healing in Your presence. Despite my prayers and the prayers of others, Your desire to have her with You prevailed. I fell to my knees in submission to Your will.

I cried unto the Lord with my voice; with my voice unto the Lord did I make my supplication.

I poured out my complaint before him; I shewed before him my trouble.

When my spirit was overwhelmed within me, then

thou knewest my path. In the way wherein I walked have they privily laid a snare for me.

I looked on my right hand, and beheld, but there was no man that would know me: refuge failed me; no man cared for my soul.

I cried unto thee, O Lord: I said, Thou art my refuge and my portion in the land of the living.

Attend unto my cry; for I am brought very low: deliver me from my persecutors; for they are stronger than I.

Bring my soul out of prison, that I may praise thy name: the righteous shall compass me about; for thou shalt deal bountifully with me.

PSALM 142:1–7 KJV

The next few services were appearances only. I stared longingly at the front pew where Mother always sat rejoicing before You, but I saw no one. The rejoicing around me did little to breach the gaping split in my heart. Mother was gone, and my prayer for healing seemed to have been denied.

Souls came to the altar awaiting my hands and arms to touch their brokenness, but my heart was overwhelmed. Who would believe that I could pray and agree with them for healing. After all, Mother had died before my eyes. Fear gripped me every time the altar call was made because I knew that many would come to seek healing.

My courage to defy the diagnosis of doctors hemorrhaged from my spirit. I could not maintain eye contact with parishioners who reached out to me for fear they would summon me.

The enemy laughed and mocked me silently before countless

thousands. "Now what are you going to do, Miss Healing Hands? Everyone knows what happened to your mother!"

My husband watched my struggle and rescued me again from my despair. He beckoned for me to come to lay hands upon and agree with a sister who had been diagnosed with a terminal disease. With every ounce of faith that I could muster, I stared death in the face and commanded it to flee in the name of Jesus!

I felt something break by the anointing of the Holy Spirit, something that had been bound. The chain that held me captive snapped and worship flooded my heart. The pain and guilt that made my cage melted in the presence of God.

Where, O death, is your victory? Where, O death, is your sting?

The sting of death is sin, and the power of sin is the law.

But thanks be to God! He gives us the victory through our Lord Jesus Christ.

Therefore, my dear brothers, stand firm. Let nothing move you. Always give yourselves fully to the work of the Lord, because you know that your labor in the Lord is not in vain.

1 CORINTHIANS 15:55–58

I looked on Mother's pew and saw that death had lost its sting and the grave held no victory. Weeks later the sister received a report of total healing. Testimony after testimony of God's healing has been shared after I stepped out of Mother's room, closed the door, and let her rest with You, Secret Keeper.

God gives us permission to forget our past and the understanding to live our present.

His truth is our shield

Because God's enemy seeks to destroy our peace, we should commune with the Lord daily about the things we're going through. He will give us wisdom and grace to do the right thing in times of trial. When we feel like the *prey,* a victim of evil pursuit, it's time for us to *pray* and take action against our predator. Prayer is the most assertive action we can take in writing a happy ending to our own life stories. Prayer gives the situation over to God to work out on our behalf. The Bible says, "You have not because you do not ask God." (See James 4:2.)

Prayer empowers you to find your own way through life without simply reacting to whatever the devil may throw at you. Prayer invites the Holy Spirit to whisper in your ears what it is the Father wants for you. Prayer establishes your faith and provides a shield around you that protects you from the fiery darts of the evil one. Prayer builds courage within your soul to say no when no is the right thing to say. Prayer keeps you aware of the loving arms of your Lord and cuts a path to victory. In another passage, God tells us what He will do for the one who depends on Him:

> He who dwells in the shelter of the Most High will rest in the shadow of the Almighty.
> I will say of the Lord, "He is my refuge and my fortress, my God, in whom I trust."

Surely he will save you from the fowler's snare and from the deadly pestilence.

He will cover you with his feathers, and under his wings you will find refuge; his faithfulness will be your shield and rampart.

You will not fear the terror of night, nor the arrow that flies by day,

Nor the pestilence that stalks in the darkness, nor the plague that destroys at midday.

PSALM 91:1–6

Notice verse 5, which reads, *You will not fear the terror of night, nor for the arrow that flies by day.* God promises psychological help for fear that creeps up on us at night and concrete help for real danger in our lives. This promise of God should revive, renew, and strengthen our hearts and minds. Trust God to give you bread for your daily journey. Ask the Holy Spirit to bring God's Word to your remembrance so that you will stand strong against the buffeting of the devil's lies. Yield yourself completely to Him and admit your need of Jesus. Then thank Him for His faithfulness.

If you feel like prey, it's time to pray!

The next time the enemy taps you on the shoulder, tempting you to look at your past, you will be able to resist him in prayer. You will ignore him and draw closer into the safety of the Father's arms. Satan doesn't like forcing you into the arms of God. When the devil sees that his flaming arrows of deceit cause you to get closer to the Father instead of deeper into retreat, he will withdraw his weapons. What a victory you will have against the enemy of God through prayer!

The word "pray" is a verb, an action word. Since English was my favorite subject in school, it made me sensitive to the sounds and meanings of words. There is an understood subject when you use a verb alone. The subject is YOU! *You* pray! *You* take action over the situation. *You* make it happen! To pray is to implore earnestly!

The homonym of pray is "prey." The noun "prey" is the person who falls victim to someone or something. The prey is the target of the game, the booty or plunder of the one who chases, the one who is about to be captured by the hunter.

So, you pray to avoid being the prey again. Take action over this situation. The dictionary defines "pray" as an appeal, to beg, to petition, and to plea. Believers know that it means to make our requests known unto God. We are to commune with Him daily about the things we're going through. The "prey," the victim, needs to commune with God, to stay in contact with God about what the hunter, the devil, is trying to do.

Are you the victim? Are your children his current target? Have your parents become the devil's prey? Or is it your ministry, your marriage, or your family? Is your reputation under fire? Pray to the Father in heaven for deliverance from the enemy, the devourer of your soul who has made you or your loved ones a target. You may have been a victim, but you are not without hope! You can pray to God in secret and He will answer you publicly. (See Matthew 6:6.)

In Psalm 91 we are reminded of what we have when we stay in constant communion with God. We are safe under His protection. It's a privilege and a comfort to know that if we abide under the shadow of the Almighty, even though the enemy comes against us like a flood, the Spirit of the Lord will lift up a standard against him. Whether it's during the storm or during the sunshine, we're safe under the shadow of the Almighty.

I will say of the Lord, He is my refuge. Others make idols their refuge—some women make their looks their refuge, and some women make money or their position in society their refuge—but we who have become prey to the enemy know that God is our refuge. God is our fortress.

The psalmist says, "In Him will I trust." There's no reason to question God's ability to keep us safe. However, the enemy keeps right on bumping up against us, making us doubt whether we're secure in God. The psalmist goes on to tell us that there is no disappointment in Him, no shadow of turning. We can be greatly encouraged with the knowledge that God's promises are sure. They're true, they're accurate, and whatever He says He'll do, He's faithful to do it. He's the only one who's not going to change His mind about us. Something can happen to us today that will alter our destiny for life, but God never changes. He's faithful and surely He will deliver us.

Our comfort is in knowing that God's promise of protection will not waver through our temptations to doubt Him. Though trying times will come, though our health may fail, though our finances may weaken, still our security is in knowing that God will not waver on our behalf. He's not worried about what we're going through. He's not nervous, anxious, or upset because He has us in the palm of His hand.

So what if the truth were known?

Anxiety in the heart of a woman weighs her down. The battle with "What if's" is a waste of time and energy.

What if my worst fear happens?

What if they find out about my past?

What if the company goes bankrupt?

What if my husband doesn't come home?

What if my daughter gets pregnant?

What if I lose my job?

What if . . . ?

Always in front of us is some type of cloud, some opportunity for anxiety over something to fear. But that possibility is what the Scriptures call the snare of the fowler. If you are familiar with hunting, you know that the snares are laid in the woods where the prey will most likely be walking. Traps are hidden so the normal eye wouldn't even see them, lest they be easy to avoid.

Often even our spiritual eye does not see the ambushments the enemy has set for us. We can be walking along and suddenly find ourselves trapped with some part of us stuck in a device that we didn't even know was in our path.

The trap may have been disguised in a relationship, an opportunity to get fast money, or a chance to go out with someone we've been wanting to know for years and years. We don't even see that it's a trap. It's set up for the prey, for the target, for the victim, and as we walk along, we don't even know that something terrible is about to happen to us. Suddenly, we are caught in the snare because we were not alert to the ways of the enemy.

The truth is, the Lord has made a way for us to escape the wiles of the enemy! Read carefully our promises defined in 2 Peter 1:2–8:

> Grace and peace be yours in abundance through the knowledge of God and of Jesus our Lord.
>
> His divine power has given us everything we need for life and godliness through our knowledge of him who called us by his own glory and goodness.
>
> Through these he has given us his very great and precious promises, so that through them you may participate in the divine nature and escape the corruption in the world caused by evil desires.
>
> For this very reason, make every effort to add to your faith goodness; and to goodness, knowledge;
>
> And to knowledge, self-control; and to self-control, perseverance; and to perseverance, godliness;
>
> And to godliness, brotherly kindness; and to brotherly kindness, love.
>
> For if you possess these qualities in increasing measure, they will keep you from being ineffective and unproductive in your knowledge of our Lord Jesus Christ.

How many times have you said, "How in the world did I get myself in this mess? I knew better! The Holy Spirit warned me!" But you let yourself be prey to the enemy of your soul. Remember, he's trying to defeat your purpose because he doesn't want you to reach the hope of your calling. But he's a liar.

It's time for the truth to be known. You need to know that no weapon formed against you will prosper! No weapon, whether you see it or whether you don't see it, will succeed in taking you out from under the protective wing of God. God will always provide the way of escape and give us everything we need for life and godliness.

You can take authority over your enemy by telling him,

> *The Lord rebuke you, Satan! You tried to defeat me, you tried to shut me down, you tried to stop me. People perish for the lack of knowledge, but be informed today that your snare won't work on me, your trap won't work on me. It won't work, because my Lord has made a way for me to escape you, just like a bird that flies through the air without a care in the world.*

God is not mocked!

The enemy would like for me to grow weary from the disappointments of my past, but I have learned that the past does not reflect the future plans God has for me. When I prayed for God to heal my mother, I did not get the answer I was wanting. But He gave me the grace to trust Him again, so that I could keep sowing faith for healing in new situations. We must trust God's sovereignty and not grow weary of doing what is right and good.

> And let us not be weary in well doing: for in due season we shall reap, if we faint not.
>
> As we have therefore opportunity, let us do good

unto all men, especially unto them who are of the household of faith.

GALATIANS 6:9–10 KJV

If the Lord delights in a man's way, he makes his steps firm; though he stumble, he will not fall, for the Lord upholds him with his hand.

PSALM 37:23–24

CHAPTER
Seven

Kick Off Your Shoes

LIFE IS LIKE A FAIRY TALE!

*Cinderella was so eager to obey her fairy godmother, she left
her beautiful shoe behind as she fled the party to be home
on time. What do you need to leave behind in order
to be obedient to God's plan for you?*

*E*verything Cinderella had ever hoped for was given to her, but
there was one condition: She needed to be home by midnight.
Even the princess in the fairy tale was given instructions that
she was expected to obey.

I said in the beginning of this book that I am setting out to
prove that life is like a fairy tale when we put our trust in God.
He guarantees that we will live happily ever after in heaven, and
if we obey Him in this life, we can expect blessings today as
well. He sets before us the choice to love and obey Him. When
we do, He promises to work all things together for our good.
(See Romans 8:28.)

The proof of this promise was greatly tested when my

husband and I suffered injuries from a deadly car accident. Here is the story of when I was a barefoot princess.

She wore one shoe

If the Lord delights in a man's way, he makes his steps firm;

though he stumble, he will not fall, for the Lord upholds him with his hand.

PSALM 37:23–24

Dear Secret Keeper,

Anyone other than a family member who passed by and saw me sitting on the floor in front of my closet that day would have thought, "She must be straightening her shoes." But my family would have thought, "Oh no! She has fallen! What in the world is she doing in the front of her closet sitting with her shoes?" But only I knew how long I had lain in my bed, staring at the ceiling, rehearsing the words I had heard, "She can only wear one shoe."

Nearly six months had passed, and the car accident seemed as though it were yesterday. The sound of the sirens still rang in my ears as I recalled watching the emergency rescue team make certain that my husband, my mother, and my two-year-old twin boys were all okay. I had never before heard the term "jaws of life," but the team who had been dispatched to remove us from the car called for them.

It was as if I were watching a movie. Right before the impact, I saw the Jeep approach the intersection and prepare to make its turn. Surely they saw us. Certainly they won't make that turn right in front of us.

*But they did! My husband's cherished Silver-Anniversary
Edition Trans-Am plowed into the front of the Jeep. The bat-
tery from our car was projected like a bullet through the air. My
husband's head cracked the windshield. My mother's shoe landed
on the folded dashboard from the backseat of the car as she cradled
the boys in her arms. The trim around the stereo knobs dangled
like hoop earrings.*

*My husband beat against the door on the driver's side in an
attempt to open it, disregarding the blood that trickled down his
face. He kept urging me, "Get out of the car!"*

*I whispered to him that I couldn't. Before I knew it he had
climbed through the bucket seats into the backseat, forced the passenger door open and stood by to assist us out. The boys were jumping up and down with the excitement only children can manifest.
Mother, somewhat shaken, stood nearby while my husband stared
with disbelief at my right foot. As he lifted me from the car he saw
the blood oozing from my ankle where the bone protruded.*

*Upon closer scrutiny, the ambulance attendant saw that my
entire heel cap had been dislocated to the side of my foot. Without my saying a word, the nearly unbearable pain that I felt was
evidenced by the tears that streamed down my face. They whisked
me into the back of the ambulance with my husband up front
peering at me through the window.*

*I felt the jolt of every pothole in the highway. They seemed
to appear from nowhere to add more agony to my pain, as if it
were possible. On the stretcher in the hall of the emergency room,
I laid for what seemed like years. Nothing and no one could have
ever prepared me for the words that the doctor on call spoke to my
husband. He lifted the sheet, and with compassion of an ice cube,
informed us that I would never walk again!*

For the Lord is good and his love endures forever;
his faithfulness continues through all generations.

PSALM 100:5

Never is a long time when you lie in bed month after month after month. You confront many issues when your faith comes to trial, and you ask many questions. How will I take care of my family? How will I be attractive to my husband? Do I really want to be a burden? Will I ever feel like a woman again? The voice of the tormentor affirmed anything and everything that would deflate my ego. And I accepted his words that added to the defeat of my self-esteem.

I could not walk without crutches. With crutches, my spirit still could not walk. As the months of recovery passed, each phone call from heartless congregation members who easily dismissed me from their presence intensified my feeling of rejection and helplessness. Whoever I was to them hindered their need for constant attention from their pastor, who happened to be my husband.

Then came the day when I lowered myself from the bed to the floor and began to scoot on my bottom toward the closet. My journey took some time because the path I had so often walked seemed longer through teary eyes. "Never walk again! Never walk again!" This was the music that paced my nonambulatory cadence. My destination was my closet floor. I began to pull from the pile of pumps and sandals my right shoes. I lined them up in front of me and to each side. The one shoe represented my destiny: Never to walk again; if so, with a metal brace and a cane.

I would have to wear one shoe.

(Now in earlier times in Israel, for the redemption and transfer of property to become final, one party took off his sandal and gave it to the other. This was the method of legalizing transactions in Israel.)

RUTH 4:7

My husband interrupted my pity party. He extended his hand to me as I sat on the floor wallowing in depression. I stood resting against his strong chest as his heart beat with his love for me. In my ear he whispered my hope for the days to come. He assured me, "If you never walk again, I will push your wheelchair, and I will never leave your side."

This man had written on my cast, "The steps of a good man are ordered by God." That day was the first day of my deliverance. His love for me insisted that I close the mouth of the enemy who was robbing me from believing God for my healing. My hero stepped back from me and took my hands. He looked from his tears into mine and said, "Just take one step."

With the agility of an elephant, I picked up my foot and it landed like a club. My hero told me that I had "done good."

"Take one more step. That's good!"

"Take another step. Now rest."

Every day my hero would hold my hands and, with loving therapy, applaud my efforts to move my club foot. He fought the enemy of our marriage for my restoration. My steps began to turn into brief walks from the chair to the couch and from the couch to the table.

In a matter of time, love lifted me! My husband, my pastor, my friend, taught me how to walk again!

Since ancient times no one has heard, no ear has perceived, no eye has seen any God besides you, who acts on behalf of those who wait for him.

ISAIAH 64:4

My confidence and my dignity were gradually restored. I returned to the tasks that I am so very fulfilled in doing: caring for my family. Every now and then, I have trouble with my ankle. But I am so thankful for the reminder of the Lord's miraculous healing power.

When I left my shoe, the Prince of Peace found it and placed it on my foot.

Today I can wear beautiful shoes again. There were times during my recovery when other women we knew made cruel jokes about my crutches. I felt ashamed of my unattractive gait and single shoe, but I learned that I could walk barefoot in the presence of my Lord and my lover whom God had given to me.

Take off your shoes

When Moses stood in the presence of God on the mountain, God told him to take off his shoes because he was on holy ground. (See Exodus 3:5.) Perhaps God didn't want anything to separate Moses from His presence. Don't you think it's time to get rid of whatever keeps you from walking into the presence of God?

The story of Ruth and Naomi illustrates a wonderful truth that surpasses the make-believe of Cinderella. Ruth began her life in hardship, like the princess in our fairy tale, but she inherited all the land upon which she once walked barefoot.

Look at her story in the book of Ruth.

During a time of famine in Bethlehem, Elimelech took his wife Naomi and his two sons to the country of Moab. His sons were named Mahlon (meaning "invalid") and Chilion (meaning "pining") who took wives after their father died. The wives, Orpah and Ruth, lived with their husbands and Naomi for about ten years until their husbands also died.

Naomi decided to return to her homeland and encouraged her daughters-in-law to go back to their homes to find husbands to care for them. But the young women didn't want to leave her. Eventually, Orpah heeded Naomi's advice and returned to her parents, but Ruth said, "I can't leave you. Don't even ask me to leave you because, wherever you go, I will go, and where you lodge, I will lodge. Your people shall be my people, and your God, my God. Where you die, there I will be buried. The Lord do so to me, and more also, if anything but death parts me from you." (See Ruth 1:16–17.)

So one daughter went back to who she used to be, and the other one, even though it meant going to a strange land, decided to follow Naomi. Ruth loved Naomi and felt that this woman could teach her the ways of her God.

God does not want us to prove ourselves but to prove Him.

When Naomi and Ruth arrived in Bethlehem, Ruth said, "Let me glean from the field of your wealthy kinsman, in whose sight I might find favor." (See Ruth 2:2.) So Naomi bid her to go. Ruth asked permission to glean in the fields after the reapers had passed through. She came early in the morning and worked with only a little rest.

When Boaz, the owner of the field, saw Ruth he told her to glean in his fields and offered her both protection and water when she was thirsty. At his demonstration of kindness, she fell on her face, bowing to the ground before him, and asked, "Why have I found favor in your eyes that you should notice me, when I am a foreigner?"

Boaz said to her, "I am fully aware of all you have done for your mother-in-law since the death of your husband and how you have left your father and mother and the land of your birth to come to a people unknown to you before. May the Lord recompense you for what you have done, and a full reward be given you by the Lord, the God of Israel, under whose wings you come to take refuge." (See Ruth 2:8–12.)

Boaz invited Ruth to eat with his reapers and made sure that she was allowed to glean where there was plenty of grain left. She continued to work in his fields until the end of the harvest. Naomi, recognizing Boaz as next of kin, instructed Ruth on how to approach Boaz with her request for their continued protection.

When Boaz became aware of Ruth's request, he blessed her for the loving-kindness she continued to show her mother-in-law. He pointed out that she could have become the wife of any man she sought, rich or poor, but she wanted someone who would also look after her mother-in-law. What Boaz said to Ruth is very important for all of us daughters of the King of Kings to understand. He said,

Fear not. I will do for you all you require, for all my people in the city know that you are a woman of strength (worth, bravery, capability).

RUTH 3:11 AMP

Ruth was a noble woman whose humility lifted her to great honor. She could have returned to her homeland and quickly married someone who would provide for her. She could have married a young man in Bethlehem and left Naomi to fend for herself. But Ruth served her mother-in-law and offered to serve Boaz as his maidservant in exchange for protecting and providing for Naomi.

Ruth's humility did not belittle her, but elevated her position to the highest level that a woman in Bethlehem could hold. She followed Naomi and the God of Israel. In so doing, she moved from being the wife of an invalid to the wife of the man who owned the fields she had walked upon. She was brave, capable, and highly valued, yet willing to serve her mother-in-law, her God, and her fellowman. She was the great-grandmother to King David, ancestor of Jesus.

Submit to protection

Let's look again at ways we can learn from Ruth. We can learn how to approach both our Lord and our lovers. When she approached Boaz, she asked him to spread the corner of his garment over her, because he was her nearest kinsman and her rightful redeemer. *The Amplified Bible* says that she asked for his wing of protection over her.

Today's society has pushed for women to become independent

and self-serving. Independence was never God's original plan for women. He wanted us to be totally dependent upon Him. Eve's attempt to find wisdom apart from His guidance was the reason she fell from His grace.

Ruth demonstrated the highest act of godliness that a woman can present to her Lord. She said, "Please help me, for it is not good for me to be alone." God does not want us to prove *ourselves* but to prove *Him*. His ways confound the world because His Word demonstrates that truth is the opposite of what the world teaches.

In chapter 4 of the book of Ruth, Boaz carefully followed the law in order to legally take Ruth as his own. There was another kinsman who had more right to her than he did, so he presented himself to the other kinsman first. The first heir forfeited his right and confirmed the promise by giving Boaz his sandal. The covenant of passing the sandal to the other symbolized the promise, "I will not tread upon your territory."

Then Boaz went to the elders and told them of his intent. This is where Boaz received a blessing because of Ruth. They said to him,

> We are witnesses. May the Lord make the woman who is coming into your home like Rachel and Leah, who together built up the house of Israel. May you have standing in Ephrathah and be famous in Bethlehem.
>
> Through the offspring the Lord gives you by this young woman, may your family be like that of Perez, whom Tamar bore to Judah.
>
> RUTH 4:11–12

The elders saw that good things were in store for Boaz if

he took Ruth as his wife. Through her willingness to submit to the council of Naomi, the protection of Boaz, and the plan of God, Ruth brought blessing even to you and me. She helped to continue the line of Jesus Christ.

Jesus continues to spread His wing over us

Do you see the parallel of Boaz and Ruth to what Jesus has done for us? When we came to the Lord and submitted ourselves to His protection, He could grant our petition because He had followed the law to legally win the right to be our Redeemer. He confronted Satan, who had first right to us because of the fall, with the price He had paid for us, and Satan could not object. He looked at Jesus and said, "I cannot tread upon Your territory."

We are under the protection of our Kinsman Redeemer, Jesus Christ. Why would we ever want to live our life apart from Him? Why would we ever want to prove our independence from the very one who loves us more than His own life? We are the Bride of Christ, heirs to the kingdom of God. We walk as heirs on ground owned by the one who owns the universe!

Kick off those painful, high-heeled shoes, Princess, and enjoy the feeling of holy ground beneath your feet!

> Brothers, I do not consider myself yet to have taken hold of it. But one thing I do: Forgetting what is behind and straining toward what is ahead, I press on toward the goal to win the prize for which God has called me heavenward in Christ Jesus.
>
> PHILIPPIANS 3:13–14

CHAPTER
Eight

Stay Till the Ball Is Over

LIFE IS LIKE A FAIRY TALE!

*Not wanting to miss the fireworks at the end of the night,
Cinderella stayed to the very last second of the celebration.
Have you been leaving the party too soon? Is there
someone you could encourage to come with you?*

Cinderella was not eager to leave the ball. She stayed until she
heard the last stroke of midnight, fearing she would miss seeing
what the Prince would do next.

I look forward to the day when women are able to stay until
the dance is over. So many of us rush from one place to another,
always having our mind on where we need to be next instead of
where we are. There is a place of rest in God that He wants us
each to attain. Once found, we will be equipped to pass on our
faith to others. As I said earlier, serving others as Jesus serves
us is the goal of our Christian walk.

If we stay with the Lord, enduring to the end of His great

plan for us, we will enjoy the rest that results from living in the kingdom of God.

The Lord gives us keys to endure, keys that unlock doors to our future and lock doors to our past that we do not want to enter into again.

Let us not be as Lot's wife who did not want to leave her home, even though her life was filled with disgusting invasions of evil. She was like a Cinderella who wanted to stay in the cinders. Remember how Lot's family was so reluctant to leave that God sent angels to pick them up and set them down outside the city before He destroyed it? (Genesis 19:16). They were warned, "Don't look back!" but Lot's wife could not see the future for her past. She disobeyed, and turned to look at her past.

Archeologists have determined that an earthquake and an explosion of gases were the probable cause of the destruction of these vile cities. The Dead Sea now covers the cities that could not be saved from God's judgment. There is no outlet to this sea and the high concentration of salt kills all life in that area. Salt rocks surround the area that were most likely the result of the rain of salt that took place during the destruction of this place. Lot's wife is entombed within one of these pillars as a silent reminder to all of us who are tempted to look back.

Endure to the end

A wonderful reward is offered to those who endure to the end. Jesus said, *Since you have kept my command to endure patiently, I will also keep you from the hour of trial that is going to come upon the whole world to test those who live on the earth* (Revelation 3:10).

There is no reward for turning back to the rags and cinders. Great sorrow and disappointment await those who turn down their invitation to the wedding supper of the Lord. Luke recorded the warning of Jesus in chapter 17:24–35:

> For the Son of Man in his day will be like the lightning, which flashes and lights up the sky from one end to the other.
>
> But first he must suffer many things and be rejected by this generation.
>
> Just as it was in the days of Noah, so also will it be in the days of the Son of Man.
>
> People were eating, drinking, marrying and being given in marriage up to the day Noah entered the ark. Then the flood came and destroyed them all.
>
> It was the same in the days of Lot. People were eating and drinking, buying and selling, planting and building.
>
> But the day Lot left Sodom, fire and sulfur rained down from heaven and destroyed them all.
>
> It will be just like this on the day the Son of Man is revealed.
>
> On that day no one who is on the roof of his house, with his goods inside, should go down to get them. Likewise, no one in the field should go back for anything.
>
> Remember Lot's wife!
>
> Whoever tries to keep his life will lose it, and whoever loses his life will preserve it.

I tell you, on that night two people will be in one bed; one will be taken and the other left.

Two women will be grinding grain together; one will be taken and the other left.

Will you still be grinding grain on the great day when the Lord returns for His bride?

Lock the door to your past!

Forgiveness is the key for locking the door to your past so that you never return to it. Unforgiveness reopens the door to yesterday's pain every time you entertain it. Unforgiveness causes you to spend all your creative time reliving the torment of the enemy's deception against you. As long as there is unforgiveness in your heart, the devil doesn't even need to bring new accusations against you. As long as he sees that you are still dressing in your graveclothes, the devil knows he can move on to other victims and leave you alone in your misery.

At first, forgiveness is difficult, but it is absolutely essential for a princess to learn how to maintain this virtue in her life. I took my weakness and laid it once again before my Secret Keeper, admitting to Him that I needed both His deliverance and protection from the painful addiction of unforgiveness. I identified with Paul's letter to the Philippians:

Brothers, I do not consider myself yet to have taken hold of it. But one thing I do: Forgetting what is behind and straining toward what is ahead,

I press on toward the goal to win the prize for which God has called me heavenward in Christ Jesus.

All of us who are mature should take such a view of things. And if on some point you think differently, that too God will make clear to you.

Only let us live up to what we have already attained.

Join with others in following my example, brothers, and take note of those who live according to the pattern we gave you.

For, as I have often told you before and now say again even with tears, many live as enemies of the cross of Christ.

Their destiny is destruction, their god is their stomach, and their glory is in their shame. Their mind is on earthly things.

But our citizenship is in heaven. And we eagerly await a Savior from there, the Lord Jesus Christ,

Who, by the power that enables him to bring everything under his control, will transform our lowly bodies so that they will be like his glorious body.

PHILIPPIANS 3:13–21

Dear Secret Keeper,

I know that I should have gotten over these feelings by now. How could everyone be going on with their lives when I feel like a car stalled on a six-lane highway during rush hour? It's hard to believe that anyone could wrestle with unforgiveness and still be Spirit-filled. But it does happen to the best of us. Harboring unforgiveness is far more damaging than what the perpetrator ever did to me.

It seems as though I am the only one left rehashing the past. It is not that you wish anyone ill will, it is just a gut-wrenching feeling that you get when someone who caused you to question your self-worth never acknowledges the injustice they have done to you. They could walk in and a sunny day would instantly disappear, as if a storm would erupt any moment. Perhaps they don't dignify your feelings with memories of the words they smirked about in corners of restaurants, on phone lines that stretched across the city, or while motoring across the country.

Surely, if they knew that I was privy to their conversations it would result in a series of apologetic incantations. Sometimes, I just wanted to walk up to them and ask out of curiosity, "Why did you make me the brunt of your heartless babble?" And right before I'd open my mouth and insert my foot, You'd tap me lovingly on the shoulder and remind me that I was looking back at days too distant to retrace.

What felt in my heart like yesterday had mysteriously turned into years. It was high time that I went on with my life. Everyone that I am lamenting over has. I need to stop memorializing past pain. It is virtually impossible to drive forward and look backward.

You intended to harm me, but God intended it for good to accomplish what is now being done, the saving of many lives.

GENESIS 50:20

After all, it did not prevent You from having the ultimate say-so in my life. It was time for me to relinquish past hurt and the ghost that held me prisoner so I could take hold of the realities only found by walking hand in hand with You into my destiny. You taught me to use maladies for stepping-stones.

The whisperings they did about me somehow became silent as they watched You prepare a table for me. The one they labeled as "Least Likely to Succeed" felt like the "Teacher's Pet."

Bear with each other and forgive whatever griev-ances you may have against one another. Forgive as the Lord forgave you.

COLOSSIANS 3:13

It now seems so uncomplicated to wear my coveted title. All of my contenders have disappeared. I now believe with my whole heart that unforgiveness involves only two. It does not matter how many voices there were that made folly of me and my dreams. When it came time for true deliverance, You and I strolled through hall after hall, past faces that had forgotten me and what they'd said. You led me to doors that stood propped open with bitterness and resentment, and I released the handles. I walked out with only the vapors of what used to be tears.

Secret Keeper, the joy of it all is that You never share with others how you had to tarry with me when I wallowed in the bed of unresolved issues. You sounded the alarm and insisted that I get up and go on. I never want to oversleep and miss what You have awakened me for.

Forgiveness is the only lasting deliverance. Others can pray that your life will improve, but only you can forgive those who have hurt you. Forgiveness breaks the power of sin and pulls down walls that separate us from God and others. Jesus taught,

> If you forgive men when they sin against you, your
> heavenly Father will also forgive you.
>
> But if you do not forgive men their sins, your Father
> will not forgive your sins.
>
> MATTHEW 6:14–15

What if forgiveness was a habit with you?

It excites me to imagine a church full of women who make
it a habit to forgive others. How would the habit of forgiveness
change us? How would it change our world?

Children would see the principle of unconditional love demonstrated from their parents. Husbands and wives would enjoy
the security of knowing that no matter what happens, there is
someone at home who will lift them up when others have cast
them down. Employees would face each new day with enthusi-
asm, eager to work as unto the Lord, having already forgotten
the offenses of the day before. It would be like having God's
will on earth as it is in heaven.

Choose to endure. Lock the door on your past. Endure to
the end and stay for the whole party that God has planned for
us. Enduring to the end means staying with God's plan long
enough to see its reward for your life and its influence on the
lives of others.

Are you Naomi, Ruth, or Orpah?

I believe there are three kinds of women who are reading
this book. You could be like Naomi, Ruth, or Orpah. Most likely,
we all identify somewhat with all three of the women. They all

understood what it was to lose everything. They had to leave behind their old churches, their old lifestyles, and their old way of doing things. Through faith, two found a new life better than their biggest dreams, but one lacked courage and retreated to her old way of life.

I hope you are not embracing the attitude of Orpah, who returned to her past and missed what God could have taught her through Naomi. Orpah would have learned everything Naomi taught Ruth, but she could not seem to grasp the vision of new possibilities in God because she was so tied to where she had come from and who she used to be. The unknown intimidated her, and she retreated to the safety of her corner.

Perhaps you are like Ruth, who was eager to learn from Naomi. Women like Ruth will initiate a healthy attachment to women like Naomi, vowing to be teachable and do whatever their mentor tells them to do. Ruth could see that this older woman could teach her the ways of the Lord. With tenacity, she implored Naomi to let her stay at her side and learn from her. She could see gifts in Naomi that Naomi couldn't even see in herself at the time.

If you are like Ruth, you are fully aware that you have more to learn. Find a woman with the qualities of Naomi and learn from her. Let her know that you admire her and need her instruction. Naomi demonstrated the ability to move when it was time to move. She did not let the disappointments of life consume her. Even though she struggled with sorrow to the point of telling everyone to call her Mara (which means bitterness), I find it interesting that everyone continued to call her Naomi. She must have demonstrated more optimism than she was aware of. Who do you know who is like that?

Forgiveness is the key for locking the door to your past so that you never return to it.

There are women who are born to be leaders and mentors, as Naomi was to Ruth. One can look at this "Naomi type" of woman and say, "When I grow up, I want to be just like her." If you already enjoy your title of princess and have learned to lock the door of your past, won't you step forth to help the next generation of young women inherit their titles? Please step forward and help the younger Christian women lift their chins with dignity again and act like daughters of the living God.

Perhaps God is prompting your heart with names of young women who would love to receive a call or a letter of encouragement from you. Perhaps you know that it is time for you to teach others how to dress for God's best as Naomi did Ruth. You will find a new love of life just as Naomi did when she took Ruth's precious baby in her arms and enjoyed being his nursemaid. Ruth told Naomi she needed her, but we can see that the teacher also became the benefactor of her student.

God wants women to build up other women:

Likewise, teach the older women to be reverent in the way they live, not to be slanderers or addicted to much wine, but to teach what is good.

Then they can train the younger women to love their husbands and children,

To be self-controlled and pure, to be busy at home,
to be kind, and to be subject to their husbands, so that
no one will malign the word of God.

TITUS 2:3–5

If you are a Naomi, you may not even recognize your
gift, but younger women will come to you and ask you for
advice. If this is happening, it is because they see wisdom
in your actions and fruit in your life. Ruth and Orpah could
both see that Naomi loved her husband. When her husband
died, Naomi grieved because everything she had dreamed of
seemed to be over.

Naomi was so devastated by the loss of her husband, she
felt she was no longer able to do anything. Are you like Naomi?
Have you given up on your own goals because the person or
thing that you associated your success with is no longer with
you? It could have been your husband. It could have been your
job. It could have been an association with people from a pre-
vious ministry or from your other way of life. Have you given
up on leading other women into victory because you've made
mistakes yourself?

The body of Christ needs women who are like Naomi. Where
are you? We need women who know God intimately and who
plan to do exploits in spite of the opposition and circumstances.
We need women who won't give up on their ministries even
though they have fallen and everybody knows about it. We need
women who will assume their rightful position as mothers in
the house of God.

Naomi must have looked at those girls and seen herself,
both what she had been and what she could have been. In loving

them, she did not manipulate or try to control them. She was careful not to deny them their right to choose to be who they were supposed to be. She encouraged them to pursue their own destinies.

We must not live our lives only for ourselves, but realize that the decisions we make are being observed by the Ruths, the Orpahs, and our daughters. We need to endure doing the right thing, so that God's glory is manifested in our churches. As younger women in the faith see the fruit of our decisions, they will want to follow the godly standards they see in us.

Mentorship is not teaching with words but by example. Nagging, berating, and ridiculing young women will cause them to look back instead of forward. We must practice carrying ourselves with grace and humility if we want our daughters to be trained to carry themselves like royalty.

Let the younger women hear us praise our husbands publicly. They don't want to hear us swearing at the men in our lives. Young women need to see the blessings that result in the lives of women who are submissive to their husbands. They need to be taught to lift up their husbands and help them to become godly men. They need to learn how to approach men. They need to learn how to love God with their whole heart by simply watching you.

Are the women who know you seeing Naomi or Mara? Do they see a bitter old woman who's given up on life? Could it be that Orpah only saw Mara and feared where Mara was starting to lead her? Or did Ruth say, "In spite of Noami's faults, I'm going to stick around, because God knows Naomi's life is so much better than the life I lived without God."

Be a woman who can teach new Christian women godly

character. We are about to see the greatest revival that the world has known. God is getting ready to restore women to the place that He first intended for them to be. The Church will soon be full of women who have never seen godly examples before.

There will be young Ruths and Orpahs in our midst. Oh, I hope that we will all endure to the end of the dance, and stay to help these younger women find a personal relationship with God. Please don't let them see Mara when they enter the ballroom, the sanctuary of God.

An Orpah will need lots of encouragement. She will say, "I can't do this. I love you, and God knows I've learned a lot, but I don't think I can do what you say I should do. I think I'll go back to what I'm accustomed to doing."

Will we be able to explain to her that God does the changing and all we do is the trusting? Will we have fresh testimonies that we can share with her to reveal how God cared for us yesterday just as He did so many years ago?

Were you ever on the verge of giving up because nobody took the time to tell you about themselves? Nobody took time to tell you, "Baby, God can find a wonderful man to love you and the babies you've had out of wedlock." Did anyone take time to tell you that you could lose your husband and then find a job that meets his income and your income together? Orpah won't go back to what she's accustomed to if she sees the glory of God and the testimony of His power in our lives.

We have to be willing to tell the truth. This may mean revealing some of our "secrets" so she will know that we have had hardships just as she has, but God is able to redeem all that we have lost through our sinful lives. Both the Ruths and the Orpahs need women to teach them how to wash themselves through baptism and enjoy wearing the robe of righteousness.

We will need to be honest before the young women who will be looking to us for standards. Will they think we have always been as wise as Naomi? Or will we take down the facade and admit that we have been afraid before? Will we humble ourselves and admit that we have wanted to run like Orpah did, but because we endured, we found someone who loved us when we were like Orpah?

God is moving in the world. As we lift Jesus, He will draw all men and women unto Him. We must stop lifting our own image before these young women who want to be part of the wedding dance. These women who will soon be coming to us won't be accustomed to being ladies. Like Orpah, they will come from backgrounds which were filled with religious deception, immorality, and lack of understanding about God. They won't know how to serve Him. They won't know they are walking in ungodly ways, and it will take gentleness and love to teach them the way they should go.

If you are a Naomi, the whole creation is anticipating your coming out and helping to guide the young women whom God will bring to you for help.

Where are you, Naomi? The women are dying.

Where are you, Naomi?

Please don't leave before the stroke of midnight, for there are others who need to learn how to prepare themselves for the prince. Don't go home early and redress in your cinder-covered cloak.

If you have lost interest in the party, focus on someone else who has never even been to the Lord's wedding reception. Look for the Orpahs and Ruths who need guidance in the things of God.

Teach them practical applications:

- Show them where to find those wonderful consignment stores.
- Show them the thrill of yard sales.
- Show them how to decorate one-room efficiency apartments.
- Show them how to keep their homes clean.
- Show them how to freshen themselves.

Teach them spiritual lessons:

- Show them how to wash themselves of bitterness and fear.
- Show them how to put on the garment of salvation.
- Show them how to enjoy a barefoot walk with God.
- Show them how to be first to forgive.
- Show them how to enjoy the provisions of their Father.

Don't leave too soon; there are others who need your friendship. You are not too old to be useful. You don't have too many sins in your past to be used for His glory. You haven't made too many mistakes to be a good counselor. Young women looking for love are having baby after baby, relationship after relationship;

and you could give Jesus to them if you don't go home too early.

Stay till the ball is over and help someone else learn to dance with the Lord. Teach them how to tell their secrets to the Secret Keeper. Show them that nothing is too hard for God. He can bring them out of sin and degradation. Show them the Prince of Peace who patiently waits for them.

> [You, Lord] bestow on them a crown of beauty instead of ashes, the oil of gladness instead of mourning, and a garment of praise instead of a spirit of despair.
>
> ISAIAH 61:3

CHAPTER
Nine

Sweet Dreams
Really Do Come True

LIFE IS LIKE A FAIRY TALE!

When Cinderella woke up the next morning, she thought the night before had simply been a dream. Suddenly, there was a knock at her door. Expecting to find a door-to-door solicitor, she was surprised to see her Prince waiting to be invited in. Don't you hear Him knocking at your door?

Her life would never be the same, for Cinderella had danced with the Prince. Now she knew that no one else in all the kingdom could satisfy her longing heart. She regretted fleeing from him so quickly without telling him the truth about who she was. Never in her wildest dreams did she expect him to come looking for her.

Why are we afraid to be honest with the Lord? He came to seek us out. He didn't sit on His throne and wait for us to find Him. He sent messengers ahead to let us know He was looking for us. He sent love letters to decree His intentions toward us.

Finally, He came and personally knocked on our door. Jesus didn't care that we weren't dressed up that day. He didn't care that we were wearing our cinder-covered cloak of bitterness. He loved us anyway. As soon as He saw that we were happy to see Him, He swept us in His arms and promised to never leave us. What a love story!

And it is so very true! It's not a fairy tale at all! From the beginning of time, our Father has planned this story for you to understand that *you* are the princess whom He loves. He sent Jesus to find you, to take you as His very own bride, and to live and reign with Him in a kingdom where the ways of God's loving-kindness rule. He came to take you to a place where you will never cry again, nor feel pain, nor be hungry.

We can't even imagine what that will be like. Can you remember a time in your life when you were happy? Can you remember a time when you weren't worried? Imagine feeling that way forever. The most wonderful part of this story is that it begins the day you say, "Yes, Lord, I will be Yours." He doesn't make you wait until heaven to enjoy the provisions that will someday be magnified there.

Jesus said,

> The thief cometh not, but for to steal, and to kill, and to destroy: I am come that they might have life, and that they might have it more abundantly.
>
> JOHN 10:10 KJV

The word "life" is translated from the word *zoe,* which is the same life and presence of God He breathed into Adam at creation. Jesus is saying that He came to bring us the presence of God, and not just enough for us to get by, but more than enough, so the abundance of His blessings would overflow from our lives into the lives of others.

Thousands upon thousands of women can give testimony to the provision of the Lord, but please experience His love for yourself. Let Him love you each day. When is the last time you let Him work out a problem for you? You can enjoy waking up to new mercies each morning. Jump out of bed to discover He has made your own dream for happiness come true.

Jesus can make you into a princess, and it doesn't take Him long. It may seem painful at first, because He will take things from you that you thought you had to have. But He *loves* you. He will only ask you to trade your rags for His riches. He will ask you to give Him your secrets, your filthy security blanket, and accept the radiant gown that He made just for you. What will you have to give to Him?

If you are not presently enjoying your inheritance as a princess, there is something that you need to give up in order to receive God's best for you. What is it? If you have to think about it too long, you are probably missing the obvious answer. Nothing will stand out like this memory, this person, this habit that is keeping you from accepting your blessings from God. Maybe it's your dependence on a certain relationship, a certain position at work, or certain material things that preoccupy the goals of your heart.

What have you attached yourself to so tightly that tears well up in your eyes when you think about letting it go? What is it, who is it? What ministry, what job, what pastor, what husband, what wife, what child breaks your heart when you think about letting it go and turning it completely over to God?

God won't share your heart with other idols. He will remove them from your list of "gotta-haves" and prove that you didn't have to have them after all. He will show you that you don't need it. You don't need more money, more recognition, or more acknowledgment. You only need more of Him, and He will give you the desires of your heart. What an awesome trade!

Let's see, I give Him my secret unforgiveness, lust, hatred, greed, and codependent tendencies, and He openly gives me forgiveness, love, provision, and transparency before all those who examine my life. Then they will see that I am justified—just as if I'd never done it, been it, or even wanted it. What is this love that surpasses any fairy tale that we have ever read? Doesn't it sound worth trying?

Don't turn back to your secret way of life before hearing how He can take drugs out your system and alcohol off your breath. Yes, He will put you in beautiful gowns that won't come off for strange men. He will give you a new heart that will say, "Yes, it does matter that he's married." He will give you wisdom that tells you to get off the street at three o'clock in the morning. He will give you eyes to see that the person you are looking for will come to you like a prince, not as a thief.

The new heart He gives you will direct you to peace, not to poverty. The Lord will teach you what is right and what is wrong. He will give you a way to escape from the evil that is plotted against you. He will give you the grace and power to do the right thing.

God confirms this promise in His Word:

This is the covenant I will make with the house of
Israel after that time, declares the Lord.

I will put my laws in their minds and write them on
their hearts.

I will be their God, and they will be my people.

HEBREWS 8:10

God knows your needs—not just your material needs, but
also your emotional and physical needs. He will complete the
work He has begun in you. He will teach you to walk with dignity,
as a princess. He will make you ready to marry a prince.

Fairy tales do come true!

Dear Secret Keeper,

[You, Lord] bestow on them a crown of beauty
instead of ashes, the oil of gladness instead of mourning, and a garment of praise instead of a spirit of
despair.

ISAIAH 61:3

*Life, with all of its twists and turns can be so unpredictable.
I have always loved stories where ugly ducklings become beautiful
swans. Little did I know that you were writing a similar story on
the pages of my life.*

*I was born a coal miner's daughter. In my community, known
as a coal camp, there were no big I's and little you's. Everybody
was somebody because we all knew one another. Our fathers
all worked in the same coal mine. When our daddies came out,*

all their faces were covered with coal dust. They all looked the same.

As I have grown up, I realize now that they looked more alike than the physical eye could detect. They had all experienced the same life-threatening danger that is involved in underground mining.

Side by side they risked their lives, ate out of metal lunch buckets, and provided decent homes for their families. Nearly all of the families bought groceries from the company store, which also provided the children with the latest in modest fashion.

Recently I visited the remains of the land where we played "Red Rover" until the sun bowed and gave the stage to the moon. The dirt roads seemed so broad then, accommodating our stick ball games and hopscotch courts. Today the road only resembles the path to adulthood.

The path is marked with memories of a little girl who played alone with imaginary friends and had tea parties for doll babies. My mama nursed the wounds I received from bike accidents and falls on asphalt playgrounds.

My papa taught me the rewards of allowances earned for dusting the furniture and washing the dinner dishes. And I grew up knowing the importance of earning a decent living and taking care of your family, even if it meant risking your life.

I graduated from our local high school with high honors. It is so ironic that during the commencement exercise, I led the class of 1973 in the Lord's Prayer. Off to college I went with no idea of what it was all about. I was so lonely during the early years that it is no wonder I ended up in the wrong company.

Soon the experiments began with cigarettes, alcohol, marijuana, and sex. Gee, how else could the coal miner's daughter fit in with these city slickers whom I thought had it going on?

Through it all I knew that this was not Your will for my life, Secret Keeper. I could not get high enough to avoid Your voice, Your warnings. I would go to church occasionally and feel so repentant for my wrongdoings. I would have visions of walking past Mother's door and seeing her kneeling beside her bed. I knew that sometimes she was praying for me. Her prayers prevailed through many mishaps and calamities.

Through a series of secret pal cards, I met the love of my life. From a distance I knew that he was someone I would need in my life. I was a new convert, but he was a pastor. I dare not waltz upon him lest he think I was being carnal. So I admired and observed him from afar.

Secret Keeper, he was so strong in spirit. When he spoke, the revelation of God flowed from his mouth with such accuracy that all who heard instantly received the deliverance for which they had longed. I was so awed by Your presence in his life that I knew I had to be near him every time the opportunity presented itself.

The opportunity was presented sooner than I was prepared to receive it. He came to my church for a revival! I felt like a kindergartner on my first day at school. I had just the day before mailed a card revealing my identity. And now his secret pal was no longer a secret. It was little 'ole me!

The first night of the revival I sat in the corner in the back. I could hardly distinguish the beat of the drums from the pulse of the blood rushing through my skull. I don't even know what he preached or if he preached, all I know is that he knew my name and he probably resented the sight of my invisible face.

You don't need more money, more recognition, or more acknowledgment. You only need more of Him, and He will give you the desires of your heart.

The most unfathomable thing occurred right after service. My pastor's wife decided to introduce me! I wanted to crawl under the pew and pray for the immediate return of the Lord. "Even so come Lord Jesus!" While my pastor's wife stood talking to my "no-longer-a-secret pal," she suddenly beckoned for me to come to her. The aisle seemed a mile and half long.

My hero stared at me with eyes that I knew would melt me into the carpet. As I approached him, he began to smile that smile. To me he said, "Do you know where a bachelor can get a home-cooked meal?"

I stuttered, "I'll ask my mother." Gee, I felt so numb and dumb.

The days went by quickly, turning into months. My heart was full of him. We called one another until our phone bills resembled house payments. We talked about everything, often until the sun came up. I loved the sound of his voice, the sound of his laughter, the sound of his silence. I was in love and love was in me.

I don't think that he actually proposed. But somehow his attempt was good enough for me. Our wedding was sacred. Even then, Secret Keeper, Your presence was with us. Words of prophecy came forth to sanction our union and pronounce Your blessing upon us in the years to come. Surely, it was a dream come true!

The dream was threatened when my new husband lost the best job he had ever had. The chemical plant that he worked for laid him off. What were we to do?

Trust in the Lord with all your heart and lean not on your own understanding; in all your ways acknowledge him, and he will make your paths straight.

PROVERBS 3:5–6

My husband had heard the call of the Lord to full-time ministry. Being the responsible man that he was, his first concern was to provide for his family. Backed against the wall, he now surrendered to the voice of the Lord, trusting Him as he'd never trusted Him before. He stepped out on a walk of faith where he had never trodden and began to believe God for the impossible.

The revivals were few and far between. Our income was spasmodic, but the bills were consistently over our head. We were submerged in financial waves until one by one our utilities were disconnected. At first it was just the phone, but then to the phone was added the water, to the water was added the electricity, and all the utilities were disconnected either simultaneously or at intervals too frequent to handle.

We soon started to go to my in-laws for dinner, with or without invitation, only to return to a dark home. We played games with the twins by lighting candles and sending them to bed. The innocence of a child brings glimpses of the faith that can conquer anything.

I know how to be abased, and I know how to abound. Everywhere and in all things I have learned both to be full and to be hungry, both to abound and to suffer need.

I can do all things through Christ who strengthens me.

PHILIPPIANS 4:12–13 NKJV

We sought public assistance through welfare. It was often so degrading to sit and be insulted by the social worker who seemingly mocked our circumstance. My husband began to dig ditches for gas lines to subsidize our lack of income. He would come home to little food and sometimes a boiled water bath. I never saw his countenance fall. With blisters on his hands from the shovel's handle, he would leave morning after morning, returning with generic Pampers for the twins and a humble meal of ox tails with rice and cornbread mix.

I don't know how many shovels of dirt brought us out of our despair, but with perseverance my husband dug us out. Full-time ministry rarely begins in ditches, but often in trenches. Strategically, You led my husband through the wilderness of lack to remind him of the scripture he now says with a greater conviction:

My help comes from the Lord, who made heaven and earth. He will not allow your foot to be moved; He who keeps you will not slumber.

PSALM 121:2–3 NKJV

The invitations for revivals and ministry began to come from coast to coast. The word that he spoke was revelatory and born from experience. The word held such healing for so many that it was noised abroad of the "Boy Pastor from West Virginia" who had not celebrated his thirtieth birthday.

Promotion came from You, Lord. With each revelation came the provision my husband so desperately desired for our family. From a small two-bedroom apartment to a wood-frame home to a split-level mid-entry on the side of a hill to the home that anyone would consider their dream. He disciplined himself and drove his family safely through. In my eyes, he is the greatest hero I will ever know. He taught me how to walk again.

I recall his elevation to the office of the Bishop. It was such an esteemed honor and position. We were all so proud. As I prepared his royal robes for the consecration service, I noticed how regal the purple brocade fabric was. I pressed the half cape that would cover his strong shoulders that had carried his family through financial travesty without complaint. My spirit echoed, "He is royalty. He is a prince in the kingdom. Tonight he receives the crown that will house many jewels."

A prince indeed? If this be so, could it be that I am his princess? Does this make me a princess in the kingdom? Indeed it does! Tonight You reward him openly for prayers that were prayed in his secret place to You.

Secret Keeper, I know that You were the one who dried his tears and calmed his fears. Thank You for giving me this kind, wonderful prince. I will honor him and respect him with every ounce of my being.

Here I sit, unscathed by the innumerable darts of the enemy. One night I exchanged my "Street Van" for a stretch limousine. When our chariot arrived, the doors swung open to a red carpet streaked with roving skylights. My prince, my knight in shining armor, was my husband who had been nominated for a "Grammy."

From the dirt road of a coal mining community to the red carpet rolled out for me across the world I remain the same little girl who talked to imaginary friends and hosted tea parties for doll babies. I don't know whether I was a little girl dreaming I was a princess back then, or whether I am now a princess dreaming I am a little girl. It's like an ugly duckling to a beautiful swan story. It's just like a fairy tale.

Thank You, Secret Keeper, for the promise that we can live happily ever after.

The Lord gives and grants the dream

More than all else, I hope you see by my testimonies that it is the Lord who performs the great work in you, not you who perform for Him. He has called you to an everlasting love, and He will complete the good work that He has started in you.

When He comes, your prayer may be full of unbelief:

Me, Lord? When I look at the way I was before You came into my life, I wonder, are You talking to me, God? You're loving me, Lord? Your mind is full of me? God, as holy as You are, You're talking to me, God! Not just every now and then, but on a daily basis. You've taken it upon Yourself to speak personally and distinctly and call me by my name. There was no doubt in my mind: You were not talking to somebody across the room, but You were talking to me, God!

I was not looking for the Lord the night He rescued me from my cinder-smudged face and my pitiful corner of self-pity. Everybody around me was looking at me with expressions of surprise, as if to say, "He couldn't be talking to Serita. I know God's not talking to *her*." But the Lord said to me, "Oh, yes, I called you something nobody else had ever called you. I called you unblamable, unreprovable, forgiven, washed, holy, purposeful."

Aren't we grateful to be saved, forgiven, and not forgotten? Though He forgot what we couldn't forget, He didn't forget us. He's already forgotten what we still regret. So many things happen to us during our lives that we wish we could wipe off the slate. We want to start over with a clean board so we won't have to tell our children our secrets. But the slate has been forgiven and erased. God did that for you and me, and we're the only ones who keep bringing up the past. We keep remembering who we were and who we could have been if we hadn't made certain wrong turns with certain individuals, but God is not thinking about that old girl. In the sea of forgetfulness, He's drowned her.

I can remember when I got baptized. I went to church as a favor to my mother. I thought, *Okay, I will go down there with those "sanctified folks." I'll go because I will have time to get out and do what I need to do.* And as I sat there beside my mother, God's anointing began to fall.

I wasn't accustomed to the spirit of prophecy, so when Pastor started prophesying, I was startled when He looked me right in the eye and said, "You dream a lot. You have visions of things that are going to happen before they happen. God has a call on your life."

I started trembling, because I had known there was something I was supposed to do in the kingdom. But for some reason, instead of going left, I went right. Instead of going up, I went down. And instead of listening to the voice of the Lord, I listened to the voices of my peers, those who didn't know or care what was best for me.

As I sat there listening to Pastor, I became uncomfortable. I knew this was my day for deliverance. When he said, "Who wants to get baptized in the name of the Lord Jesus?" my feet hit the floor and, before I knew it, I was up front, bent over, repenting and weeping before the Lord. Afterwards, the deacon baptized me in Jesus' name.

He kept saying, "Serita, look in the water. Whoever you were before you came to this meeting today is in the water. All of your sins are in that water. Look in that water. *Whoever* you were when you came in here, she's in the water. *Whatever* you planned to do when you left this service, she's in the water. God has put a barrier between who you were and who He has called you to be."

I looked in the water and saw dope and sex and a mess. I thought, *God, You did that for me? In a matter of fifteen minutes, You gave me a new life? How could that be? I was sick of me and You set me free.* Nothing changed outwardly. I still had problems that needed to be faced and dealt with. But my mind had changed. I knew that I was brand-new in Christ Jesus, because He had accepted me just by saying, "Yes, Lord, I am Yours." I started leaping and rejoicing.

As special as He made me feel, I am obligated and privileged to tell you that He has the same love letter for you. He's a mighty God. Appreciate Him. Thank Him. Enjoy His presence and His sweet Spirit as He fulfills His purpose in you. Pull down strongholds, cast down imaginations, and put the past under your feet.

Yet the Lord longs to be gracious to you; he rises to show you compassion. For the Lord is a God of justice. Blessed are all who wait for him!

ISAIAH 30:18

CHAPTER
Ten

A Prince Is Waiting for You

LIFE IS LIKE A FAIRY TALE!

Cinderella would never have known how much the prince truly loved her if she had continued to hide the fact that she wasn't really a princess, but was merely a servant. He changed her truth and it turned out that she was a princess after all. Have you had an honest talk with the Prince of Peace?

When the prince learned the truth, that Cinderella was poor and destitute, he was able to prove his great love for her by saying, "It doesn't matter what you have or what you have done, I love who you are. All that I have is yours, if you will simply say yes." He valued her above his own life and took her to be his bride. Together they served the people in his kingdom happily ever after.

Can't you see the parallel of Cinderella's fable to your own love story with Jesus? Only your secrets keep you hiding when He comes looking for you. He knows what you have done. He knows all about your weaknesses, but He also knows what you do not understand. He knows what the Father has in store for you, and He sees who you will become under the nurturing of His love.

Don't let your secrets create walls that separate you from God! Jesus has paid a great price to tear the veil in the temple of God that once separated us from the Holy of Holies. Remember how it used to be when only the priest could enter into the place where God dwelt? The priest had to wash and sanctify himself with water to enter the room where God was.

Now we are washed and made clean by Truth, and God enters into our very heart. Don't let secrets keep you from telling the Secret Keeper your truth. Be honest with Him and watch the walls that once kept you from enjoying the face of God fall to the ground in ruins.

We are to worship God in spirit and in truth. This means we must take off our mask. It isn't really hiding anything anyway! Take off the mask and see that you are in great company, for we all have had secrets like you. Let Him see the real you. Let Him see your pain. Let Him see your concerns. Tell Him when you are worried, lonely, or hurting. Let Him hear and see your naked, broken life and heal you with His truth.

He will not leave you bleeding on the side of the road. He will not leave you longing for somebody else to touch you. He will give you all you need. He will keep His promises. He won't leave you or forsake you. He won't give up on you. He is a friend who will always remain closer than a brother.

Pull down walls that keep you from God

I read a book by Robert Fulghum entitled *All I Really Need to Know I Learned in Kindergarten.* Fulghum suggests that serenity and a quiet spirit are very much needed in our noisy society. He tells the story of villagers in the Solomon Islands who go out into the forest, and if a tree is in the way of a path they want to take, they scream at the tree for thirty days to make the tree die and fall. Day in and day out they scream at the tree, and in thirty days the tree begins to whither and die.

Jesus taught the same lesson, that we can speak to trees that aren't bearing fruit and forbid them to live:

> And seeing a lone fig tree by the road, He came to it, and found nothing on it except leaves only; and He said to it, "No longer shall there ever be any fruit from you." And at once the fig tree withered.
>
> And seeing this, the disciples marveled, saying, "How did the fig tree wither at once?"
>
> And Jesus answered and said to them, "Truly I say to you, if you have faith, and do not doubt, you shall not only do what was done to the fig tree, but even if you say to this mountain, 'Be taken up and cast into the sea,' it shall happen.
>
> "And all things you ask in prayer, believing, you shall receive."
>
> MATTHEW 21:19–22 NASB

Are there fruitless trees in your life that need to be cursed and cast into the sea? God has given you authority to cast out the things that don't bear life for you. That is part of your inheritance as a princess reigning with Jesus in the kingdom of God.

I think Fulghum made a good point about needing serenity

and quiet. He wrote that hollering and screaming at a living thing kills its spirit. If someone or something has been screaming at you, it is time to respond. I beg to differ with the old adage that says, "Sticks and stones may break my bones, but words will never harm me." Cruel, unkind words can stay with us for the rest of our lives if we don't know how to respond to them.

If a tree can die from spoken words, how much more can unkind words kill our spirit? Fulghum listed all the different things that we might scream at during the day: the car that pulled out in front of us, our spouse, our children, and even the computer! He came to the conclusion that we need to study to be quiet, that we must learn self-control so that we do not say things hastily. Most of all, we must learn not to scream.

Perhaps there is something inside of you that needs to be shouted at. I have found that there is a time to scream at that which oppresses me! But perhaps you are screaming at something or someone you shouldn't. Perhaps there is something that makes you feel like screaming, but you can't quite put your finger on what it is.

When you are honest with yourself, what is inside of you that makes you feel like screaming? First, what is that coming out of you that makes you look like you are screaming when you enter a room? What does your posture say about you? What does your walk suggest about you? What does the way that you stare at those who are different from you suggest about you?

And who can others hear you screaming at? What makes you scream at them? Is it the employer who overlooks you? Is it your spouse, who never acknowledges your hard work? Is it your children who cannot be controlled?

What's going on inside of you that only you know about? What's buried under all that wonderful attire, that beautiful dress, that fabulous suit? What's really going on under the superficial smile that turns into tears as soon as someone walks away?

What are you screaming at? Sometimes, unbeknownst to us, others see our prejudice. They see our jealousy, our rebellion, and our indecisiveness. It can only help us if we let ourselves see it too.

What is going on with you?

Oh, Princess, that you would only learn to rest in God! If you could only learn to trust your Savior in all things:

> This is what the Sovereign Lord, the Holy One of Israel, says: "In repentance and rest is your salvation, in quietness and trust is your strength, but you would have none of it.
>
> "You said, 'No, we will flee on horses.' Therefore you will flee! You said, 'We will ride off on swift horses.' Therefore your pursuers will be swift!
>
> "A thousand will flee at the threat of one; at the threat of five you will all flee away, till you are left like a flagstaff on a mountaintop, like a banner on a hill."
>
> Yet the Lord longs to be gracious to you; he rises to show you compassion. For the Lord is a God of justice. Blessed are all who wait for him!
>
> ISAIAH 30:15–18

In repentance and rest is our salvation, yet we insist on running away on swift horses. The Lord says that in quietness and in confidence we shall gain strength, but we would not allow that to happen. Even then, the Lord longs to be gracious to us. In rest and in trust shall be our victory. When we learn to just let it go and turn it over to Jesus, He will make everything all right again.

The enemy wants you to keep screaming at your past. He doesn't want you to grow in God. He doesn't want you to reach your potential in God. He'll remind you of the people who abused you, and every time you see somebody who looks like them, something will rise up in you. At that moment, let it go! Let God arise and His enemies will scatter.

If you must scream, scream at the real enemy of your soul. The enemy is not someone who is sitting beside you. When you look in the mirror and see only the person you used to be, tell the enemy of your soul. "NO! I will not let you keep me back! I will not let you hold me down! God has great plans for me, and I am following God!"

When Joshua fought the battle of Jericho, his warriors couldn't see how beautiful Jericho was behind the wall. Palm trees grew in Jericho and it was plush and green, but no one could see it because of that wall.

What gifts and talents are you hiding behind a wall that needs to fall? What attachment are you holding onto from your past that keeps your wall standing? What if we all knew your secrets? Are you afraid we wouldn't love you? Would you still love us if you knew our secrets?

Why do we feel we have to come to church and pretend to

be somebody who God knows we're not? He knows all about us. There's nothing hidden from Him, and nothing about us offends Him or causes Him to disclaim us. He knows if our mother is a strange woman. He knows of our peculiar attachments. He knows if we didn't get a good start in life, and if we weren't presented as a debutante. He knows if we were unwed mothers at sixteen. He knows . . . but He's called us, "Jericho, beautiful, beautiful, Jericho, surrounded by a wall. You belong to Me." God claimed Jericho as His own.

God knew Jericho was beautiful

The wall of Jericho was much wider than the walls of forts we see in the movie reenactments of our Wild West. The wall around Jericho was so wide that Rahab the harlot was able to build her house in the wall itself. A community, not just her alone but her whole family, lived with her in the wall.

If we live in a wall, everyone related to us becomes entrapped in our wall. No one gets to see inside of Jericho as long as we are content to stay within its confines. Every time we are reminded of our shame, we put another layer on top of the wall. Every time someone does something to us that reminds us that we were raped or molested, or every time we see the boss who stood in our face and said, "You're nothing," another layer is added to our wall.

It's time to bring down the wall that is hiding the beauty of who you really are. Joshua was told to simply walk quietly around the wall and wait for the moment that God said to shout. We too are invited to walk quietly with our Father; and, if there is any screaming to be done, it is to celebrate that He has brought down that wall that has separated us from Him and from each other. Jesus has given us authority to trample on snakes and scorpions. There is no more worthy snake to put under our feet than Satan. Let's agree that the wall has come down.

Satan, we picket your wall, we march around the wall, we refuse to allow you to lock up the promises of God behind the wall. There is a good marriage behind the wall. The real gift of our ministry is behind the wall.

Our children will be healed when they get through the wall. Our lives will be better when we get through the wall. God has promised us Jericho. He said to be strong and courageous, for, "I am with thee, to deliver thee, whithersoever thou goest."

Operation "mission impossible" is to tear down the wall, brick by brick, course by course, line by line, memory by memory, struggle by struggle, doubt by doubt, and fear by fear. We pull down the memory of what they said, what we heard, what we went through, what happened when we were nine, what happened when we were twelve, what happened when we were thirteen.

Satan, in the name of Jesus, we are tearing down this wall. We won't live behind the walls anymore!

The anointing pulls down strongholds and destroys the yoke. The yoke isn't somewhere across the street; it's on us. We don't need to destroy a yoke next door; we need to break the yoke off our own neck, off our ministries, off our relationships, off our marriages, off our ability to love others. We can't love others or accept love when walls separate us. The name of Jesus pulls down the wall.

The enemy tried to sabotage our youth, he tried to mess us up, because he knew God wanted to use us. He tried to ruin our alpha to destroy our omega, but the devil is a liar. He knows we can't help where we've been, but we can change where we're going. We can't help how we started, but we can change how we end up. We can rewrite the ending to our own story.

The people of God got together and said, "We've seen the other side of the wall, and we're going to march around it until we get a breakthrough!" What they did seems silly, but it was a divine strategy. It came from the Captain of the host himself. For six days they marched around the wall, saying absolutely nothing at all. They just assessed the situation.

When you really get ready to be healed, you have to assess the damage. You have to look at the situation and say, "Why am I like this? Why do I keep running people out of my life? Why am I afraid people will get too close to me? Why do I shut doors on myself? Why is it that when God gets ready to use me, I can believe Him to use everybody else, but I can't believe God to use me?"

For six days they silently inspected the wall. So, take a minute right now and look to see if you have a wall that separates you from others. If so, what is holding you back from possessing what God says is yours? Take a look at it. Israel spent more time looking at the wall than they did screaming at it. For six days, they just assessed it. How did I get like this? What in the world happened to me?

No doubt there are things in your past that are so terrible you can scarcely utter them. Behind all of the pretense of maturity, most of us are battered children who grew up. We're still dealing with childish issues of rejection and abuse. But our real enemy now is this wall.

We are to worship God in spirit and in truth. This means we must take off our mask. It isn't hiding anything anyway!

If you can get through this wall, the anointing is going to rain on you. If you can get through this wall, healing is going to rain on you. If you can get through this wall, you're going to lay hands on the sick and they shall recover. If you can get through this wall, demons are going to tremble when you get up in the morning. If you can get through this wall. . . .

Perhaps you have become so discouraged with the wall that you have contemplated suicide. You wouldn't tell anybody, because it's embarrassing, but sometimes the wall has been so thick that you secretly wished you were dead. Bishop and I come together to speak life to you! You shall not die. You're going to live.

To tear down the wall and live, you will need to give the greatest offering that you have ever given. No, you won't need your checkbook to make this offering. This offering is more than money; it's an offering of *honesty*.

Honesty is an offering people hardly ever give, because we dare not admit to anyone that we're in trouble. We worry about what others might think if they knew that what they see is not who we are. Who cares what they think? The truth is, everyone else is so worried about their own secrets that they aren't even thinking about us. But we are often in trouble and yet resist the one thing that will set us free. Truth will set us free.

God wants to heal you. Won't you let His power pull down the wall?

And the wall came tumbling down

Some years ago, I was taught a term that I find most befitting for the journals I have shared with you. During a psychology class in college we were introduced to the phrase "territorial bubble." A territorial bubble is described as an invisible wall which individuals erect to shield themselves from the people with whom they come in contact. This invisible barrier causes people on an elevator to stare upward at the changing floor numbers to avoid eye contact with one another.

This bubble prevents people from getting too close to you. I would even venture to say that a territorial bubble can shield your heart from would-be intruders who seek to find out your dreams and the secrets that are hidden in your heart. The fear is that if they invade your bubble, your invisible wall, they will mock your desire to live happily ever after.

> When the trumpets sounded, the people shouted,
> and at the sound of the trumpet, when the people gave
> a loud shout, the wall collapsed; so every man charged
> straight in, and they took the city.
>
> JOSHUA 6:20

Walls, whether visible or invisible, are mechanisms of self-defense. They are used to keep the uninvited out. They ward off would-be assassins and enemies. The concept of walls is timeless. Throughout history, specifically in the Bible, walls represented safety. Some walls were so wide that communities were built on top of them. Those who resided in these communities had the strategic advantage of seeing on either side of the wall. They could see both what was hidden inside the protection of the wall and what was prevented from coming inside.

No doubt, those who resided on top of the wall longed to come down to enjoy the pleasures kept behind the wall but were too intimidated by the impending danger on the other side. How could they enjoy the beauty inside the wall, knowing that enemies lurked outside who might find a way to break in at any moment? They remained trapped on top of their fortress. Sometimes, to protect the ones I loved, I have extended them a rope to come join me on top of my wall of safety.

Recently while walking on the campus of a maximum-security women's prison where I was ministering, I was drawn to the many different walls that existed. The visible walls were obviously intimidating. They imposed such finality as they entrapped us, daring us to try to go beyond them. There were cinderblock walls and fenced walls all around me. The only way to get beyond the wall was to have an escort assigned to us that took us from point A to point B. Without instruction, I knew how far I was allowed to go.

Through a fenced wall I watched the women during what was referred to as their period of outside recreation. Some walked, some ran, and some waved and greeted us warmly. Others made enticing comments inappropriately addressed to their same sex.

Walls were all around us. I could stare at them and they at me and none of us could get out. None of us were able to get in. These walls were a direct result of one's own conduct or actions. However, the walls were reinforced by the actions of others.

I would sometimes allow people inside my self-erected walls; however, it was by invitation only. I felt compelled to protect my heart from anyone who tried to get too close to the secret place.

When you have only shared the tormented pain of the past with the Secret Keeper, you often, without realizing it, construct a wall. Like a princess in a fairy tale, you are kept in an ivory tower atop a wall, waiting for Prince Charming to rescue you from the impending doom that accompanies the hush-hush of secrets.

Many come to retrieve you, but they can only get so far up the wall. They either grow weary with their attempts to get to know you, or they tire of the invisible wall that appears without warning and often without cause.

> The Lord is close to the brokenhearted and saves those who are crushed in spirit.
>
> Psalm 34:18

What only the Secret Keeper knows is the misery that is involved in being the princess who has lost her shoe. The shoe you leave behind is such a significant part of you. It determines who you are and who you will become. Your true identity is undeniably connected to experiences in your yesterday.

Deliverance finally comes when you confront your past and put it in its proper perspective. It happened to you but *it* is not you. You survived the trauma; you too can walk again. Could it be that you are to share your secrets so that you can come from behind the wall and allow others to come in?

My husband recently took me to Jerusalem. We visited many historical sights that are so vividly portrayed in the Scriptures. Of all of the places I walked, the most impacting was when I encountered the Wailing Wall. There were tiers of history, layers upon layers. From a distance I could perceive the height and breadth of the wall. It was vast, more than the eye could encompass without panning from side to side and from top to bottom.

In front of the wall were women. Some of the women were in wheelchairs while others were in strollers. All ages and stages of life were represented. There were those who had head coverings and others who had nose rings. All of us encountered the wall for different reasons.

I thought of the studies I had done on the Court of the Women, which was situated near the entrance of the temple. The Wailing Wall flanked one side of the court. It was one of the sights frequented by the Secret Keeper, the place where He sat and observed the activities of the women.

It is said that it was the place to which the woman caught in adultery was dragged by her accusers. It could be where the widow cast in her mite. Both women's real actions were known only by the Secret Keeper, who said of one, "She has given all that she had," and of the other, "Let him who is without sin condemn her." Perhaps men saw and knew what these women had done, but the Secret Keeper knew *why* they did what they did. With this knowledge comes deliverance.

> My little children, let us not love in word, neither in tongue; but in deed and in truth.
> And hereby we know that we are of the truth, and shall assure our hearts before him.
> For if our heart condemn us, God is greater than our heart, and knoweth all things.
>
> 1 JOHN 3:18–20 KJV

You see, dear reader, when I came to the realization that the Secret Keeper had already forgiven what I could not forget and that He had already forgotten what I still regretted, there was such a release. The walls I had built to protect my feelings and to hide the guilt of the past became less and less needful. All along I felt I was keeping people from getting in, but in actuality I was prohibiting myself from getting out. An invisible wall trapped me.

Only the Secret Keeper could rescue me, and He has!

Standing at the Wailing Wall with other women who were just like me, I confronted the real wall. I began to release tears of gratefulness. Ironically, the ugly duckling in me came face-to-face with something life-altering and symbolic. Each step that I had to take to reach the wall represented memories in my life that I sorely needed to release. Instead of the wall getting smaller, with much intimidation it loomed above my head.

It was so high I could not see the top. That is how my secrets had held me captive. It is customary for those who visit the

Wailing Wall to write prayer requests on paper and press them into the cracks of the wall. Thinking of all the issues that were in my heart, I began to search for something to leave in the wall. With a tearstained face, I reached inside my purse and found my one and only business card. It was to become more than just a prayer request, because I did not need to write anything on it. It already had my name on it, and that engraving held all that the Secret Keeper had bid me to become. On the card was printed my name, Serita Ann. "Serita" is translated "Sarah," which means "princess." "Ann" means "grace," and the Lord was calling me to be "Princess Grace."

> Brethren, I do not count myself to have apprehended; but one thing I do, forgetting those things which are behind and reaching forward to those things which are ahead, I press toward the goal.
>
> PHILIPPIANS 3:13 NKJV

I folded my request and found a small opening in the wall. On this opening that held my heart's desire, I laid my head and began to worship. I lost all consciousness of those around me. More women began to move into the space I had occupied alone for so long. It didn't matter that they were close enough to hear my cry, because they were crying too.

I needed no walls to protect me from people who were basically just like me, battling shame and guilt in their minds. It was time to walk out of my past into my future. The beautiful swan had to fly. There was a princess within, and the Prince of Peace was waiting for me!

In all your ways acknowledge Him, and He shall direct your paths.

Proverbs 3:6 NKJV

I am so thankful. I don't know how or when, but dear reader, I slipped through the wall!

How to Use This Study Guide

*T*hese study questions can help you think deeply about the truths discussed in each chapter. Each of the Scriptures mentioned in the chapter has been listed along with the questions. As you read the questions, jot your answers in a prayer journal.

Chapter One: Princess, Why Are You Hiding?

Scriptures mentioned: Genesis 32:24; Psalm 34:6–7; 121:1–8; John 1:12; 1 John 1:9

1. At the beginning of the chapter, Serita asks: "Have you forfeited what your Father in heaven has written in His will for you?" How would you answer that question? Why?

2. Do you know what God's will is for your life? How has this knowledge been confirmed to you?

3. To what aspects of the princess's story do you relate the most? Why?

4. What secrets, if any, have caused you to hide? Why?

5. Serita explains, "Secrets lose their power if there is no longer a reason to hide their truths. The right secret keeper can make the person feel acceptable again." What qualities make a person "the right" sort of secret keeper?

6. What happens when we tell our secrets to the "wrong" person? Has this happened to you in the past? Explain.

7. Do you have a secret keeper? If not, why not?

8. Who is the ultimate secret keeper? Is He yours? Why or why not?

9. According to Serita, what do you inherit once you reveal your secrets? How will embracing this truth help you deal with past hurts?

Chapter Two: But Everyone Is Invited to the Party!

Scriptures mentioned: Genesis 3; Matthew 23:27–28; John 1:12; Romans 3:23; 6:23; James 1:23–24; 2 Peter 3:9; Revelation 19:9

1. Cinderella believed everyone was invited to the ball with one exception: her. Have you ever believed that an invitation was given to everyone but you? What was the invitation? How did you respond when you thought you weren't invited?

2. As Serita asks, why are we willing to be left out or willing to believe we have been left out? What is it about your past or present that causes you to feel this way?

3. Serita mentions the sense of shame that goes with being left out. Can you recall a time when you felt this way? Explain.

4. How can you RSVP to the party that God plans for His Son and the Church?

5. Why do we sometimes avoid telling God our secrets? How are we like Adam and Eve in this regard?

6. Eve chose to believe a lie about God—about His character and concern for her. What, if any, lies have you believed about God and how He feels about you? How have these lies affected your life?

7. God's question to Adam and Eve—"Where are you?"—is for you as well. Where are you spiritually? Where would you like to be?

Chapter Three: Is That Any Way for a Princess to Act?

Scriptures mentioned: Esther 1:10–22; 2:1–9; Lamentations 3:22; Romans 6:4; 10:10–11; 1 Corinthians 14:4; 2 Corinthians 5:17; Ephesians 5:18–20; James 1:23–24

1. At the beginning of the chapter, Serita asks: "Do you look forward to seeing the face of Lord?" How would you respond?

2. What is a princess's worth based upon? Do you agree? Why or why not?

3. Serita mentions that a princess does not have to gaze into mirrors to measure her worth. Rather, we should look through windows to see the needs of others. What tends to be your focus?

4. What is the mirror Serita advises you to gaze into each day? Do you? Why or why not?

5. According to Serita, what is the goal of our Christian walk? Is that your goal? How do your actions show that this is true?

6. What are the windows of opportunity in your life? What, if anything, prevents you from taking advantage of these opportunities?

7. In order to give to others, what do you need first? (Consider 1 Corinthians 14:4 and Ephesians 5:18–20.)

8. When the Lord calls, how do you respond: like Vashti or like Esther? Explain.

Chapter Four: Wash Off Those Cinders!

Scriptures mentioned: Esther 2:1–4, 8–9; 7:2–10; Zechariah 3:3–4; Matthew 10:32; Acts 1:8; 2:38; 10:47–48; Romans 6:1–8; 8:15; 2 Corinthians 12:9; Galatians 4:6–9; Philippians 4:13; Hebrews 1:3; 11:6

1. Do you or did you ever feel that you had to have your act together before coming to the Lord? Why or why not?

2. Serita asks, "Where did God's servants have to look to find us?" How did your walk with Jesus begin?

3. What public act has been provided for us as a sign that we have washed off the cinders (see Romans 6:1–8)? Have you done this? If so, briefly describe your story. Can you relate to Serita's story? Why or why not?

4. Serita advises, "Don't give God a negative résumé." Instead of a litany of negative responses, what can you say to God? Why is that important?

5. Does favor grant us an exemption from problems? Why or why not?

6. Based on the three chambers of the women known to the king, what are the three ways that we can approach God? Which of the three chambers best identifies your approach? Why?

7. What would you ask of God to do for you? Why?

Chapter Five: Put on a More Revealing Dress

Scriptures mentioned: 1 Samuel 16:7; Isaiah 61:3; Zechariah 3:2–4; John 4:4; 10–14; Philippians 2:1–17; Colossians 3:12–17; 1 Peter 5:5–7; 2 Peter 1:3

1. How do clothes affect our confidence?

2. According to 1 Peter 5:5–7, what type of "clothes" can you put on?

3. What is the difference between humility and humiliation (false humility)? Which do you have? How do your actions show this?

4. What does your day look like when you "put on Christ"? (See Colossians 3:12–17.)

5. Based on Philippians 2:1–17, what did Jesus' humility look like? How does that affect our lives?

6. After reading the story of the woman at the well (John 4), what thoughts come to mind? Are you more like the woman in the story, or like the women in town who shun her? What does Jesus' acceptance of this woman teach you? How does it make you feel?

7. For what do you thirst? Have you taken a drink of living water? Why or why not?

Chapter Six: Find Your Own Way to the Dance

Scriptures mentioned: Psalm 37:23–24; 91:1–6; 103:11–12; 142:1–7; Matthew 6:6; 1 Corinthians 15:55–58; Galatians 6:9–10; Hebrews 8:10–12; James 4:2; 2 Peter 1: 2–8

1. Serita asks, "Whose permission are you waiting on [before you can enjoy your inheritance]?" How would you answer that question?

2. Why is forgetting the past necessary to be able to enjoy "the ball"? Are there any regrets from the past that are keeping you from embracing the life God has for you? Explain your answer.

3. How has the enemy tried to "keep you in the cinders of who you were"?

4. How has prayer helped you in the past?

5. What do you need to tell God—your Secret Keeper—right now about your situation?

6. Are you feeling victorious, or more like "prey"? What does Psalm 91 suggest?

7. What are the "what ifs" that haunt you? What would you tell God about them?

Chapter Seven: Kick Off Your Shoes

Scriptures mentioned: Exodus 3:5; Ruth 1:16–17; 2:2, 8–12; 3:11; 4:7, 11–12; Psalm 37:23–24; 100:5; Isaiah 64:4; Romans 8:28; Philippians 3:13–14

1. Serita mentions that we can expect blessings from God. Is that easy or hard for you to do? Why?

2. Based on your current situation, what encouragement do you find in Psalm 37:23–24 or Romans 8:28?

3. Take a second look at the story of Serita's accident. Even if you haven't been in an accident of that type, can you relate to how she felt during her period of recovery? Why or why not? Do you see any parallels to your situation? Explain.

4. Is there anything keeping you from walking into God's presence right now? Explain.

5. What strikes you most about Ruth's story? Is there anything about her situation that you wish were true of your life? Why?

6. What does Ruth's story teach you about approaching God? Your loved ones?

7. If you are a believer, you are under Jesus' protection. How does that make you feel about your situation?

Chapter Eight: Stay Till the Ball Is Over

Scriptures mentioned: Genesis 19:16; 50:20; Isaiah 61:3; Matthew 6:14–15; Luke 17:24–35; Philippians 3:13–21; Colossians 3:13; Titus 2:3–5; Revelation 3:10

1. Who, if anyone, would you invite to "the ball" (to become part of the kingdom of God)?

2. What is the reward of enduring till the end (staying with God's plan)?

3. Is it easy or hard for you to forgive the past? Explain.

4. Why do you think Serita refers to God's deliverance as "the only lasting deliverance"?

5. How would the habit of forgiveness affect your world?

6. Of the three kinds of women (Ruth, Naomi, and Orpah), with whom do you identify the most? Why?

7. Who are the Naomi's in your life? To whom are you a Naomi?

8. Who are the Orpahs and Ruths in your community? What can you teach them?

Chapter Nine: Sweet Dreams Really Do Come True

Scriptures mentioned: Psalm 121:2–3; Proverbs 3:5–6; Isaiah 30:18; 61:3; John 10:10; Philippians 4:12–13; Hebrews 8:10

1. Serita asks, "Why are we afraid to be honest with the Lord?" How would you answer that?

2. What is your happiest memory? As Serita mentions, imagine feeling that way for all eternity. Is it easy or hard to believe that life can be like this all of the time? Explain.

3. What do you think the "abundant life" described in John 10:10 means?

4. What does your "security blanket" look like? How is that blanket helping or hindering your life?

5. What do you need to give to God right now in order to enjoy your inheritance?

6. Take another look at Serita's "coal miner's daughter" story. To what aspects of her experience do you relate the most?

7. What dreams are you hoping the Lord will grant in your life?

Chapter Ten: A Prince Is Waiting for You

Scriptures mentioned: Joshua 6:20; Psalm 34:18; Proverbs 3:6; Isaiah 30:15–18; Matthew 21:19–22; Philippians 3:13; 1 John 3:18–20

1. Have your secrets created a wall between God and you? Why or why not?

2. If you answered yes, what do you think it would take to knock down that wall?

3. What, if any, are the "fruitless trees" of your life?

4. Serita asks, "What is inside of you that makes you feel like screaming?" How would you answer that question?

5. Is there anyone at whom you're screaming? Explain.

6. What keeps you from accepting the rest offered by God?

7. Are there any walls behind which you are hiding your gifts and talents? Explain.

8. Have you taken the time to assess your situation in order to receive healing? How do your actions show that you have?

9. What, if any, are the "territorial bubbles" in your life?

10. Serita refers to the mistakes/traumas of the past or the guilt of those events as the "shoe" that was left behind. What is your "shoe"? How will honesty about your shoe break down the walls erected around your life?

How to Use This Study Guide

These study questions can help you think deeply about the truths discussed in each chapter. Each of the Scriptures mentioned in the chapter has been listed along with the questions. As you read the questions, jot your answers in a journal so that you will be ready to participate in your group's discussion.

For the Group Leader

Encourage the women in your group to come prepared to discuss what they have read. Make the group a safe place for all to participate by reminding them that what is talked about in your group stays there. While you want everyone to participate in discussions, be sensitive to those who might prefer to remain silent at times. Or if one or two women tend to dominate the conversation, you can redirect the question to someone else. For example, "Thank you, Candace, for your thoughts. Now let's hear what some others have to say."

For each session, suggestions for optional video clips and prayer points have been provided.

To introduce the topic, icebreaker questions have been provided.

Group Icebreaker Questions

Show a clip from Disney's *Cinderella* or *Enchanted*.

1. What are your favorite fairy tales?

2. Why are they your favorites?

3. Why are fairy tales so enduring?

Chapter One: Princess, Why Are You Hiding?

Scriptures mentioned: Genesis 32:24; Psalm 34:6–7; 121:1–8; John 1:12; 1 John 1:9

Show a clip from Disney's or Rodgers and Hammerstein's *Cinderella*. You might show any scene at the beginning where Cinderella's dreary life with her stepmother and stepsisters is described.

1. At the beginning of the chapter, Serita asks: "Have you forfeited what your Father in heaven has written in His will for you?" How would you answer that question? Why?

2. Do you know what God's will is for your life? How has this knowledge been confirmed to you?

3. To what aspects of the princess's story do you relate the most? Why?

4. Serita explains, "Secrets lose their power if there is no longer a reason to hide their truths. The right secret keeper can make the person feel acceptable again." What qualities make a person "the right" sort of secret keeper?

5. What happens when we tell our secrets to the "wrong" person? Has this happened to you in the past? Explain.

5. Do you have a secret keeper? If not, why not?

7. Who is the ultimate secret keeper? Is He yours? Why or why not?

8. According to Serita, what do you inherit once you reveal your secrets? How will embracing this truth help you deal with past hurts?

Take a few minutes to pray about any secrets the women feel led to share.

Chapter Two: But Everyone Is Invited to the Party!

Scriptures mentioned: Genesis 3; Matthew 23:27–28; John 1:12; Romans 3:23; 6:23; James 1:23–24; 2 Peter 3:9; Revelation 19:9

Show a clip from Disney's or Rodgers and Hammerstein's *Cinderella*. You might show the scene where the invitation to the ball is given.

1. Cinderella believed everyone was invited to the ball with one exception: her. Have you ever believed that an invitation was given to everyone but you? What was the invitation? How did you respond when you thought you weren't invited?

2. As Serita asks, why are we willing to be left out or willing to believe we have been left out?

3. Serita mentions the sense of shame that goes with being left out. Can you recall a time when you felt this way? Explain.

4. How can you RSVP to the party that God plans for His Son and the Church?

5. Why do we sometimes avoid telling God our secrets? How are we like Adam and Eve in this regard?

6. Eve chose to believe a lie about God—about His character and concern for her. What, if any, lies have you believed about God and how He feels about you? How have these lies affected your life?

7. God's question to Adam and Eve—"Where are you?"—is for you as well. Where are you spiritually? Where would you like to be?

Take a few minutes to ask God for healing concerning any lies that have been believed.

Chapter Three: Is That Any Way for a Princess to Act?

Scriptures mentioned: Esther 1:10–22; 2:1–9; Lamentations 3:22; Romans 6:4; 10:10–11; 1 Corinthians 14:4; 2 Corinthians 5:17; Ephesians 5:18–20; James 1:23–24

Show a clip from Disney's *Snow White*. You might show any scene where the queen gazes into the mirror.

1. At the beginning of the chapter, Serita asks: "Do you look forward to seeing the face of Lord?" How would you respond?

2. What is a princess's worth based upon? Do you agree? Why or why not?

3. Serita mentions that a princess does not have to gaze into mirrors to measure her worth. Rather, we should look through windows to see the needs of others. What tends to be your focus?

4. What is the mirror Serita advises you to gaze into each day? Do you? Why or why not?

5. According to Serita, what is the goal of our Christian walk? Is that your goal? How do your actions show that this is true?

6. What are the windows of opportunity in your life? What, if anything, prevents you from taking advantage of these opportunities?

7. In order to give to others, what do you need first? (Consider 1 Corinthians 14:4 and Ephesians 5:18–20.)

8. When the Lord calls, how do you respond: like Vashti or like Esther? Explain.

Take a few minutes to pray, committing to respond to the Lord's call like Esther.

Chapter Four: Wash Off Those Cinders!

Scriptures mentioned: Esther 2:1–4, 8–9; 7:2–10; Zechariah 3:3–4; Matthew 10:32; Acts 1:8; 2:38; 10:47–48; Romans 6:1–8; 8:15; 2 Corinthians 12:9; Galatians 4:6–9; Philippians 4:13; Hebrews 1:3; 11:6

Show a clip from Disney's *Cinderella.* You might show the scene where Cinderella is looking at her ragged dress while her fairy godmother tries to hurry her into the carriage. (This is just before the fairy godmother realizes that Cinderella is still in rags.)

1. Do you or did you ever feel that you had to have your act together before coming to the Lord? Why or why not?

2. Serita asks, "Where did God's servants have to look to find us?" How did your walk with Jesus begin?

   Give a few who wish to share their faith journey a few minutes to briefly do so.

3. What public act has been provided for us as a sign that we have washed off the cinders (see Romans 6:1–8)? Have you done this? If so, briefly describe your story. Can you relate to Serita's story? Why or why not?

4. Serita advises, "Don't give God a negative résumé." Instead of a litany of negative responses, what can you say to God? Why is that important?

5. Does favor grant us an exemption from problems? Why or why not?

6. Based on the three chambers of the women known to the king, what are the three ways that we can approach God? Which of the three chambers best identifies your approach? Why?

7. What would you ask of God to do for you? Why?

Take a few minutes to pray silently, giving the women an opportunity to talk to God about their responses to question 7.

Chapter Five: Put on a More Revealing Dress

Scriptures mentioned: 1 Samuel 16:7; Isaiah 61:3; Zechariah 3:2–4;John 4:4; 10–14; Philippians 2:1–17; Colossians 3:12–17; 1 Peter 5:5–7; 2 Peter 1:3

Show a clip from Disney's (or any version of) *Cinderella*. You might show the scene where Cinderella's fairy godmother is about to clothe Cinderella in a beautiful gown.

1. How do clothes affect our confidence?

2. According to 1 Peter 5:5–7, what type of "clothes" can you put on?

3. What is the difference between humility and humiliation (false humility)? Which do you have? How do your actions show this?

4. What does your day look like when you "put on Christ"? (See Colossians 3:12–17.)

5. Based on Philippians 2:1–17, what did Jesus' humility look like? How does that affect our lives?

6. After reading the story of the woman at the well (John 4), what thoughts come to mind? Are we more like the woman in the story, or like the women in town who shun her? What does Jesus' acceptance of this woman teach us?

7. For what do you thirst? Have you taken a drink of living water? Why or why not?

Take a few minutes to seek God for a sip of living water.

Chapter Six: Find Your Own Way to the Dance

Scriptures mentioned: Psalm 37:23–24; 91:1–6; 103:11–12; 142:1–7; Matthew 6:6; 1 Corinthians 15:55–58; Galatians 6:9–10; Hebrews 8:10–12; James 4:2; 2 Peter 1: 2–8

Show a clip from Disney's or Rodgers and Hammerstein's *Cinderella*. You might show the scene where Cinderella's fairy godmother turns the pumpkin into a coach.

1. Serita asks, "Whose permission are you waiting on [before you can enjoy your inheritance]?" How would you answer that question?

2. Why is forgetting the past necessary to be able to enjoy "the ball"? Are there any regrets from the past that are keeping you from embracing the life God has for you? Explain your answer.

3. How has the enemy tried to "keep you in the cinders of who you were"?

4. How has prayer helped you in the past?

5. What do you need to tell God—your Secret Keeper—right now about your situation?

6. Are you feeling victorious, or more like "prey"? What does Psalm 91 suggest?

Take a few minutes to pray for those who are feeling like "prey."

Chapter Seven: Kick Off Your Shoes

Scriptures mentioned: Exodus 3:5; Ruth 1:16–17; 2:2, 8–12; 3:11; 4:7, 11–12; Psalm 37:23–24; 100:5; Isaiah 64:4; Romans 8:28; Philippians 3:13–14

Show a clip from Disney's or Rodgers and Hammerstein's *Cinderella.* You might show the scene where Cinderella leaves a shoe behind at the ball.

1. Serita mentions that we can expect blessings from God. Is that easy or hard for you to do? Why?

2. Based on your current situation, what encouragement do you find in Psalm 37:23–24 or Romans 8:28?

3. Take a second look at the story of Serita's accident. Even if you haven't been in an accident of that type, can you relate to how she felt during her period of recovery? Why or why not? Do you see any parallels to your situation? Explain.

4. Is there anything keeping you from walking into God's presence right now? Explain.

5. What strikes you most about Ruth's story? Is there anything about her situation that you wish were true of your life? Why?

6. What does Ruth's story teach you about approaching God? Your loved ones?

7. If you are a believer, you are under Jesus' protection. How does that make you feel about your situation?

Take a few minutes to pray for a stronger realization of Jesus' presence.

Chapter Eight: Stay Till the Ball Is Over

Scriptures mentioned: Genesis 19:16; 50:20; Isaiah 61:3; Matthew 6:14–15; Luke 17:24–35; Philippians 3:13–21; Colossians 3:13; Titus 2:3–5; Revelation 3:10

Show a clip from Disney's (or any version of) *Cinderella.* You might show the scene where Cinderella and the prince are dancing or lingering in the garden.

1. Who, if anyone, would you invite to "the ball" (to become part of the kingdom of God)?

2. What is the reward of enduring till the end (staying with God's plan)?

3. Is it easy or hard for you to forgive the past? Explain.

4. Why do you think Serita refers to God's deliverance as "the only lasting deliverance"?

5. How would the habit of forgiveness affect your world?

6. Of the three kinds of women (Ruth, Naomi, and Orpah), with whom do you identify the most? Why?

7. Who are the Naomi's in your life? To whom are you a Naomi?

8. Who are the Orpahs and Ruths in your community? What can you teach them?

Break into small groups and take a few minutes to pray for the Naomis, Orpahs, and Ruths in your congregation.

Chapter Nine: Sweet Dreams Really Do Come True

Scriptures mentioned: Psalm 121:2–3; Proverbs 3:5–6; Isaiah 30:18; 61:3; John 10:10; Philippians 4:12–13; Hebrews 8:10

Show a clip from Disney's (or any version of) *Cinderella.* You might show the scene where the palace official tries the slipper on Cinderella's foot and it fits. (In the Rodgers and Hammerstein version, the prince actually comes to Cinderella's house.)

1. Serita asks, "Why are we afraid to be honest with the Lord?" How would you answer that?

2. What is your happiest memory? As Serita mentions, imagine feeling that way for all eternity. Is it easy or hard to believe that life can be like this all of the time? Explain.

3. What do you think the "abundant life" described in John 10:10 means?

4. Do you have a "security blanket"? If so, how is that blanket helping or hindering your life?

5. What do you need to give to God right now in order to enjoy your inheritance?

6. Take another look at Serita's "coal miner's daughter" story. To what aspects of her experience do you relate the most?

7. What dreams are you hoping the Lord will grant in your life?

Take a few minutes to pray for the dreams mentioned in answer to question 7.

Chapter Ten: A Prince Is Waiting for You

Scriptures mentioned: Joshua 6:20; Psalm 34:18; Proverbs 3:6; Isaiah 30:15–18; Matthew 21:19–22; Philippians 3:13; 1 John 3:18–20

Show a clip from Disney's (or any version of) *Cinderella*. You might show the scene where Cinderella and the prince are finally married and are running from the church.

1. Have your secrets created a wall between God and you? Why or why not?

2. If you answered yes, what do you think it would take to knock down that wall?

3. What, if any, are the "fruitless trees" of your life?

4. Serita asks, "What is inside of you that makes you feel like screaming?" How would you answer that question?

5. Is there anyone at whom you're screaming? Explain.

6. What keeps you from accepting the rest offered by God?

7. Are there any walls behind which you are hiding your gifts and talents? Explain.

8. Have you taken the time to assess your situation in order to receive healing? How do your actions show that you have?

9. What, if any, are the "territorial bubbles" in your life?

10. Serita refers to the mistakes/traumas of the past or the guilt of those events as the "shoe" that was left behind. What is your "shoe"? How will honesty about your shoe break down the walls erected around your life?

Take a few minutes to pray for the walls we erect around our lives. Ask God to break down those walls.

About the Author

$\mathcal{S}$erita A. Jakes has been involved in Christian ministry all of her adult life and has served alongside her husband, Bishop T.D. Jakes, throughout their marriage of nearly thirty years. As an insightful speaker, she draws heavily from her education and background in theater and mass communications. A soft-spoken woman offstage, First Lady Jakes, as she is affectionately referred to by The Potter's House congregation, possesses the rare ability to reach and stir her audiences as she works to complement her husband's ministry.

In addition to raising three sons and two daughters, she has assumed an active role at The Potter's House of Dallas, where her husband serves as Senior Pastor. First Lady Jakes serves as Executive Director of the church's Woman-to-Woman women's ministry. She is founder of the much-acclaimed God's Leading Ladies Life Enrichment program for women and The Potter's House's Debutante Program for teenage girls. Mrs. Jakes also speaks across the country on women's roles in supporting their husbands, and she is in demand by women's organizations nationwide as a celebrated speaker on issues concerning marriage and family. First Lady Jakes and her husband founded Clay Academy, a private college-preparatory Christian school. In addition to *The Princess Within*, her books include *Beside Every Good Man: Loving Myself While Standing by Him*.

With echoes of her husband's preaching style, Mrs. Jakes boldly challenges women to serve as blessings to their husbands and families. The Potter's House family attributes Mrs. Jakes' wisdom and leadership to the emphasis she places on a close personal relationship with God.

The Jakes family makes their home in Dallas, Texas.

You can contact First Lady Serita Ann Jakes at

T.D. Jakes Ministries, Inc.
P.O. Box 5390
Dallas, TX 75208

214–333–6315

www.tdjakes.org

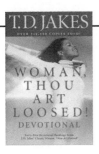
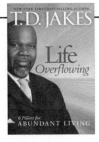

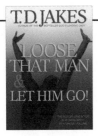
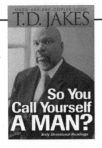